Raising Donkeys

The Ultimate Guide to Donkey Selection, Caring, and Training, Including a Comparison of Standard and Miniature Donkeys

Contents

Introduction

Donkeys are unique creatures that evolved and adapted to live in harsh environments with rough terrain and without a lot of nutrient-rich forage. This makes them hardy animals and good for a variety of agricultural and other types of physical tasks. Many use donkeys as guard animals for livestock; others use them to carry small loads on their backs or to pull carts. They can provide manual labor for grinding stones and even make their way between narrow rows of produce with more ease than a horse.

Many people keep donkeys as pets or companion animals. Raising donkeys can be a lucrative and rewarding experience that provides a decent income. They are incredibly strong and have a great temperament, and are less expensive to purchase and care for than horses. Their smaller size makes them suitable for tasks that horses cannot perform.

Like with any animal, though, there is care involved, and these animals must receive regular care and maintenance to thrive. Knowing what all donkey ownership entails and how to care for your animals is the point of this guide.

What This Guide Contains

First, we briefly introduce the social and evolutionary history of the donkey - from their time in the wild to human's early use of them for a variety of labor functions. Then, we will touch on some of the major breeds, temperament, physical differences, and the like. Next, we will move on to tips and information you need to purchase healthy animals that meet your expectations and needs.

Training and Management

Once we have gotten through the basic information you'll need, we will turn to the care of donkeys, including feeding and maintenance, such as grooming and hoof care. You'll learn the best ways to train donkeys with tips and hints on how to get the success you desire in this process is provided in detail. Everything you need to know about donkey breeding is reviewed. Common diseases and issues that can plague donkeys, how to avoid these problems, and how to diagnose them are also covered.

We then have a brief aside on the milking of donkeys, which isn't all that common but *perhaps should be.*

Finally, we round out the book with a discussion of mules and end with information about how to create a business raising and caring for donkeys.

Chapter 1: Purpose and Benefits of Raising Donkeys

Donkeys and Humans: A Longstanding Relationship

Donkeys have first domesticated some 6,000-years ago and have had a long and beneficial relationship with humans ever since. Known scientifically as Equus asinus and descended from an African wild ass, they have been a well-loved work animal since early in human civilization. Males are called jacks, females as a jenny or jennet, and their offspring as a foal. They have served several purposes for humans during their long history with us, including companion animals to other farm animals, protection, riding, and even as a work animal or beast of burden.

The donkey has a long and storied history alongside humanity and is a great animal to have with other equines, like horses. Interestingly, donkeys can also mate with several other equine species, including horses and zebras. Their offspring are called hinny or mules and zedonk (or zebrass), respectively.

This humble and unique animal was also prized for its working power and even healing power. For a long time, donkey milk was used as a medicinal substance for a variety of circumstances. This included feeding premature babies, sick children, and there is even evidence it was thought to be an effective treatment for tuberculosis patients. Their milk is higher in sugar and lowers in fat than cow's milk.

Like other equine, donkeys are also long-lived animals. They tend to live to at least 25-years old, and it's not unheard of for a donkey to live as long as 60 years in some cases. At 40, a donkey would be considered elderly and thus unable to work with the same vigor and ferocity as a younger donkey can.

Benefits of Donkeys

There are a lot of misconceptions about donkeys that may make one think that they don't make good animals for pets or as a farm animal. However, they have a huge number of positive behaviors and traits that make them highly desirable as farm animals, whether for their power to work or their power to protect. Let's take a look at some of the biggest benefits of raising donkeys on your property.

Temperament

Donkeys get a bad rap for being stubborn, which is largely not true. They are highly intelligent animals that learn and react in different ways than, say, a horse might. They can be taught several valuable behaviors and tend to be gentle – even affectionate –animals that show a wide range of positive social skills, both with people and other animals. They have a good attitude about most things, and unless they feel threatened, they tend to be rather quiet animals. This means, if your donkey is braying loudly, there is probably something afoot.

Especially when gotten as foals (babies), they will often grow up to be sweet and affectionate towards people. They are very social and will need a lot of social interaction with both people and animals, and they can even be taught to eat out of your hands. Donkeys get on well with other donkeys and horses (particularly mares) and can be taught to tolerate other animals like cows, sheep, goats, etc. While they will bond with livestock, it is important to understand that they are territorial animals.

When introducing a donkey to livestock, it needs to be supervised to ensure the safety of the stock animals, as donkeys can be extremely aggressive if they feel threatened. Most often, the process of introduction takes place over several weeks and starts with a fence or some sort of guard between the donkey and the stock animals. Once the donkey is used to the stock animals, they will typically be gentle and friendly towards them.

Since they are so social, they can develop deep bonds with people or other animals. This means they can experience great distress if a companion animal dies. Though rare, this can, in extreme cases, lead to a condition called hyperlipemia, which can even cause death.

Donkeys also do prefer a calm and quiet environment. Loud noises and a lot of rackets are likely to stress or irritate the animal, and they have been known to bite the animal or person who is the source of loud noises - something to remember if children are going to be around the donkey.

Intelligent

Donkeys, like other equine species, are known for their intelligence. They are highly curious creatures who can learn a wide range of different behaviors and reactions to stimuli. They not only crave, but they also need mental stimulation and can act out and develop unwanted behaviors if they aren't given enough space or ways to fill their time. Like humans, they act out when they are bored.

Since donkeys are such social creatures, they thrive best when raised with other animals, particularly donkeys or mares (female horses). They are also less likely to develop undesirable behaviors when raised with adult animals like other donkeys who have been properly raised. It seems they can learn both good and bad behaviors from other animals.

While they are incredibly intelligent, it is important to note that there are sharp distinctions between them and humans. They do not possess a "moral compass," nor do they take cues from their social surroundings as to what is or is not acceptable behavior. In short, they don't know the difference between right and wrong, as that is a human construct. This is something to remember when training a donkey.

A donkey simply responds to what works or doesn't work, not whether the action or behavior is desirable or wanted. The type of reinforcement you give the donkey is key, and they learn much better with clear and simple communication from the trainer or owner. As with most animals, unnatural behaviors, such as being ridden, take longer for a donkey to learn. They will pick up on their surroundings much faster, making it easier for them to learn proper interactions with other animals. With this in mind, you must stay patient when training a young donkey.

As the owner or trainer gets to know the donkey, both will learn to better "read" each other. The way an owner or trainer treats the donkey will have a huge impact on how well and how quickly they learn to do desirable behaviors. Again, communication is key, and donkeys with a good rapport with their trainer or owner tend to pick up new skills more quickly.

Horses are well known for having highly expressive body language, which can give owners and trainers clues as to the mindset or emotional state of the animal. This isn't the case with donkeys, and it can take longer to get to know and understand the actions and behaviors of the animal. To many, they are "hard to read" when it comes to their emotional state, and they've been said to have a very stoic temperament that gives little emotion away. This doesn't at all mean they don't have emotions - they most certainly do - it just takes longer and is more difficult to ascertain.

Since they can be a little hard to read, this can cause some miscommunication between animal and owner or trainer. Since humans best understand human body language, we can often misread a donkey's behavior in ways that don't apply to the animal. For example, sometimes, when a donkey is highly stressed, their eyes will widen. To a human, this may indicate curiosity and interest, but it is a sign of distress.

Their cool demeanor is also why so many people use them as guard animals, though this might be surprising to some at first. They are less prone to the "flight reaction" than horses and other equines, which means they are more likely to stand up to predators. This lowered flight reaction makes them stand their ground in potentially threatening situations, which will be discussed in more detail below.

You'll get to know your donkey's personality better with time, which will lead to more effective and positive interactions and communications with the animal. As you learn about their personality, you can learn better to communicate your wants and desires to the animal, and they are more likely to understand what you want from them. Like humans must get to know each other to have effective communication, so to do humans and donkeys.

Being social and highly intelligent, donkeys make great animals for younger people or others with limitations to learn to ride. They can also be put to work in a variety of ways, which is discussed below.

Behaviors

As intelligent creatures, donkeys can exhibit a huge array of different behaviors and can learn how to perform several tasks, but some of their natural behaviors should still be understood. Donkeys are known for being pretty "chill" creatures. One reason many people choose them over horses is that they tend to have a calmer and more laid-back demeanor. They are also curious, gentle, and will often be affectionate with trusted humans.

Training is key for achieving desired behaviors and minimizing the expression of undesirable behaviors. Patience is important when training a donkey. The adage that they are stubborn is not as true as some might think, but it definitely has some merit. Since they are social creatures, they will feed off signals we give them, whether intended or otherwise. It is vital that trainers know their body language and verbal cues they may be giving to the animal, as this will affect how well (or not well) they pick up the behaviors one is attempting to teach them. Good or desirable behaviors need to be rewarded and encouraged quickly.

Their behavior is reliably stable, so any dramatic or noticeable change in behavior may be an indication of a larger problem. If the donkey is acting markedly different than normal, it is recommended to have them looked at for potential health issues. If they start to develop an undesirable behavior, address it immediately, as the behavior is more likely to be expressed (and harder to eliminate) the longer it is allowed to continue.

While we do know a lot about donkeys, there is still a lot we don't know. For example, there is a question as to whether behavioral traits can be passed from one donkey to another; right now, the proverbial jury is still out on that one. Since a lot is unknown about their genetics, but we do know that their surroundings and environment are largely indicative of their behavior and attitude, how they are raised becomes ever more important.

Trainers will have the best results in terms of the donkey's interaction with and relations to other animals when they are socialized from a young age with other animals. They learn for their surrounding environment, and so only trained animals that exhibit the desired behaviors should be kept with a donkey in training. Often, donkeys are kept with mares and foals. Well-trained mares will help create the environment for a well-trained donkey. It is vital to start interacting with them and working with them at a young age.

Behaviors are far more difficult to get rid of once they emerge rather than reduce the likelihood of their occurring, to begin with.

Donkeys can also be very vocal when they want to communicate something, and, though it will take time, you will learn what the different noises mean or what emotions they indicate. This will also help you more effectively communicate with your animal and determine what is wrong in the event the animal is showing distress.

Chewing is an incredibly common behavior for donkeys. They are known to chew on anything from wooden fence posts to items of clothing that may have been left around. They are also known to escape, so keeping fences properly closed and latched is also important.

Environment

Donkeys can live in a wide range of different environments and terrains, which can make them more versatile than other equines with more limited environmental requirements. If, for example, you live on difficult or uneven terrain, a donkey is an option much better than a horse as they can more easily navigate an uncertain environment and are far more nimble.

The donkey evolved and selectively bred to withstand long journeys with scarce forage for them to eat. This means they can function on far fewer resources than, say, a horse can. Due to the environment they evolved in, they are lean but also amazingly smart and cunning, able to find food to browse on even in seemingly inhospitable environs.

In the wild, it is easy for a donkey to stay trim and fit, often hailing from the desert or other harsh types of environment where there simply isn't enough food for them to become overweight. However, if they are given too much access to food or forage as farm animals, they can easily become overweight, and a lot of negative health problems can result from this. A strict feeding schedule is recommended, and they require little supplemental feeding if provided a decent amount of area to browse.

Donkeys also evolved to be highly active animals and thus require a decent amount of physical and mental stimulation, or they may begin to act out or show signs of mental distress. They need to have a proper amount of space to move about it.

They also aren't that great with changes, particularly large environmental ones. While these changes cannot always be avoided in certain circumstances, it is important that, if possible, any change is introduced slowly to allow the donkey to acclimate.

Low-Maintenance

One of the most important reasons to own donkeys is that they are relatively low maintenance, especially when compared with other equines known for having finicky dietary needs and often requiring lots of veterinary care. They tend to be healthy, robust animals that rarely have issues. Not that donkeys can't get sick or never experience negative health, but comparatively speaking, they are far less hassle than a horse.

Donkeys require a lot fewer inputs than other equines. They can largely browse for their food and need only a little supplemental hay or straw to get by. They also eat, by volume, far less than horses and other equines, which makes them an economical choice for sure. They are also not nearly as expensive from the outset. They are well known to require less food than even an equally-sized pony.

As grazing animals, donkeys will eat almost any fiber-rich vegetation and can find sufficient nutrition off a relatively small plot of fallow land. Since they can eat nearly anything, they find much of their nutritional needs from wild foods. They may browse vegetation for up to 16 hours a day. They prefer browsing on higher fiber plants, but as stated above, just about any vegetation is fair game. Each animal requires about a half-acre of land in order to graze.

They need a bit supplemental hay only or straw, most often in winter, when forage is harder to come by. They will need regular access to water and do drink more than some other equine animals. They thrive best when given daily trace mineral salts, which will be discussed in depth in the chapter on feeding.

Donkeys are hoofed animals, like all other equines, and thus, at times, will require foot maintenance. They do not get nearly as many feet issues as horses are known to get but will require hoof trimming about every 4-8 weeks. And the donkey will also need to be regularly drenched (dewormed). Like most equines, they will require regular vaccination against things like influenza, and when this basic care is provided, they rarely need any more medical treatment than this.

Unlike horses, donkeys do not have an undercoat. This leaves them more vulnerable to rain and cold and will require protection from the elements.

Protection/Companionship

The donkey is growing in popularity as a companion animal due to its highly social and affectionate nature. They tend to be calmer and laid back than horses and will often become so affectionate with people as to eat from their hands and greet them when they come into their living space. While they may be a little stubborn when it comes to learning new things, they really do tend to be quiet, gentle animals, but at times, donkeys will snap at other animals for being too loud or to protect their environment if they feel threatened.

Not only do donkeys make good companions for people, but they also make even better companions for other animals. They get on very well with other equines, including mares and foals. They are often introduced as a companion to a horse mare after her foals are taken from her. They almost always get on well with other donkeys, especially if they are raised from foals together.

Perhaps less commonly known is the highly territorial nature of donkeys, which is both a positive aspect of this animal and can be a downside. It's positive in that they will protect flocks and can even run off predators if they feel their environment is threatened. They have huge ears and are known for their great hearing, so they will often hear any potential intrusions well before any other animal and certain people.

They don't distinguish, and dogs may be included in animals that are run off from the yard. If they are raised with puppies, they will be more used to them and, thus, will be less likely to bite them. However, they are famous for nipping to keep an unruly pup in line. And it should also be said that all donkeys are different, and some simply won't abide by a dog, any dog, regardless.

Due to their highly territorial nature, donkeys can be used to guard livestock like sheep, goats, cows, and the like. However, the introduction needs to be gradual. As we noted earlier, donkeys don't like a drastic change, and they are territorial, so they have to be introduced to new animals slowly. This often takes place during several weeks, first through a fence or some other form of protection, then supervised, until finally the donkey can be left alone with the livestock.

To the donkey, the livestock simply becomes part of its environment. While they will most certainly protect the livestock in their territory, they are more protecting the territory than the animals, though the result is the same. Though it takes time, the donkey will often bond with the other animals and spend much of its time browsing near the rest of the crew.

Donkeys won't bother with small animals like birds or raccoons, but they will run off dogs, foxes, and coyotes. They are always listening and amazingly attentive to their surroundings; they often investigate unknown noises or commotion. Unlike horses, donkeys are not as prone to running at signs of a potential threat. They will stand their ground and even attack if running the interloper off isn't successful. Kicking and biting are their two most common forms of defense. They will also use auditory threats like loud braying.

If possible, it is best to raise the donkey with other animals in the area. Then, it is less likely to ever turn against the family pet or livestock, and the animal will bond more solidly with the livestock.

Here, we should point out that intact jacks are not the best choice for this purpose. Most often, jennies or gelded (castrated) jacks are used for guarding and protection purposes.

Work

During their millennia-long partnership with humans, donkeys have been prized for their low maintenance and ability to work. Donkeys are very hard-working animals, and though not as common today, they were once the primary work animal in several, largely inhospitable environments. Their hardiness and ability to work in rough conditions is part of what made them so attractive to man all those thousands of years ago.

Though many keep them today as companion animals, donkeys are great to work animals and can provide for several functions. As we mentioned briefly earlier, donkeys can be great to ride. This is especially true for children, older adults, or those with disabilities. Donkeys, of course, are not large and intimidating, have a good demeanor, and are often less scary to young children than horses. Most important of all, donkeys are very patient, which is huge for teaching a child to ride. Since they are so gentle and often affectionate, they just interact better with children besides being a more reasonable size to ride.

Though riding is what they are most used for in a work setting today, they are also great to pack animals and can even haul small loads in carts. They can carry up to 100 lb. on their back and can pull twice their body weight at ground level, for example, using a cart.

Chapter 2: Donkey Breeds: Standard vs. Miniature

As with many animals, there are a lot of subspecies, or breeds, of the donkey, ranging in size, color, temperament, ability, and more. The word "donkey" is an English term that is most often used, as it would stand to reason, in English-speaking parts of the world. The word "burro" is another commonly used term to refer to animals in the Equus asinus genus, and it derives from the Spanish word "borrico," which simply means "donkey." Many people in non-English speaking parts of the world use the term burro to refer to miniature donkeys. In the American southwest, it is becoming increasingly common to hear donkeys called burros.

The American Donkey and Mule Society use the term "burro" to refer to mid-sized animals who descend from wild species of donkey and don't use it in relation to miniature donkeys or exceptionally large breeds. This semantic difference can cause a little confusion, depending on the origin of the website, book, or person you are talking to. Their place of origin is likely to affect the terms they use to refer to this animal.

Donkeys have been selectively bred for thousands of years to bring out a variety of features or behaviors. Predecessors to this species can still be found in the wild in many places, though they are becoming increasingly rare. Domesticated standard donkeys have been known to escape and revert to a more wild or feral state, living out their days in the wild.

Miniature donkeys are fully-domesticated animals and are not found in the wild and would not fare particularly well if they escaped.

Estimates suggest there are 50 million donkeys worldwide, making them a popular equine species though many are unfamiliar with their use as work or companion animals.

History and Types of Donkey

As stated in the opening chapter, humans have a longstanding relationship with the donkey that goes back some 6,000-years. This long history has seen a lot of change not only in human culture and society but in the look and temperament of the donkey. The different breeds of donkey will vary in size, color, and temperament, but the general history of the donkey is roughly the same regardless of breed.

A Brief History of the Donkey

Donkeys are equine species, and millions of years ago, the donkey, the horse, and other equine species all descended from the same ancient animal. Their genetic paths have diverged greatly since then, but they are distant relatives in the genetic family tree. Horses and donkeys, though related, have very different biology and temperament, so the similarities end at the fact that both are hooved equine species.

Donkeys have two distinct genetic lineages. These lineages evolved in quite different climates, and their differences are very important to their temperament and the care they need. The main lineages are Asiatic and African, which we will look at, in turn.

The Asiatic lineage of donkeys includes several species, but they all came from roughly the same area between the Red Sea and Tibet. This is a huge demographic range with vastly different environmental conditions. Asiatic donkeys evolved to deal with a huge range of environments, from a more typical desert environment to high altitudes and unsteady terrain, such as what is found in Tibet. There is a range of different species derived from the Asiatic ass.

The African lineage doesn't include as many species and covers a large, but more environmentally similar ecological niche. African asses are found between the coast of the Mediterranean Sea to the south of the Red Sea, usually in incredibly dry regions like the Sahara Desert. The two African species are the Nubian and the Somali wild ass. This is the lineage of most modern domesticated donkeys.

Donkeys have been domesticated for some 6,000 years, and it is believed that domestication originated in North Africa. The animals were originally domesticated for meat, milk, and hides. They weren't used as beasts of burden until about 2,000-years ago, at least from the evidence we have found.

The domesticated asses first used as draught animals were put to work, making the long 4,000-mile journey across the Silk Road, loaded down with cargo. This journey, since done on foot, could take a couple of years to complete. This long-distance travel resulted in breeding between disparate breeds that were once geographically far apart, helping to create the complicated assortment of donkey varieties we see in modern times.

Their use for carrying cargo on the Silk Roads exposed other peoples to their myriad of uses. The Greeks found that donkeys were ideal for traversing the narrow and rocky paths that make up the Greek lands and are small enough to navigate between grape vines - grapes being a very important part of Greek life and economics. Since they were such a good animal for working grapevines, the donkey spread to other wine-growing regions like Spain. While it seems like an unbelievably long distance, somehow getting from Africa to Spain, the coast of Spain and the coast of North Africa are only a few miles apart in certain areas.

We can thank the Romans for the entry of the donkey into mainland Europe. The Romans used donkeys for farm work, typically using them as agricultural inputs or to haul produce. Wherever the Romans would plant vines in the places they conquered, which is basically wherever they would grow, the donkey was brought. There were vineyards as far north as Germany and France during the empire.

When the Romans invaded England, they also brought the donkey along with them. Historians dated this introduction to around 43 AD when the Romans invaded Britain. While there were a few scattered donkeys in use in this area at the time, it wasn't until the 16th century that they became commonplace in the British isles.

With the invasion of Ireland by Oliver Cromwell, more donkeys were introduced into the area to assist with the war effort. They weren't used as the primary animal of burden, but they were able to make up for the shortfall of horses with their labor. It is estimated that there were some 250,000 donkeys owned by the British Army at the end of the first World War, showing just how useful they proved to be for the military.

With a long and storied history, evolving and being selectively bred alongside humans as they developed more and more complex and global civilizations shows just how close the relationship is between the evolution of the donkey and human intervention.

Standard Donkey Breeds

There are tons of different breeds of donkey. According to country reports tallied by the International Domestic Animal Diversity Information System within the Food and Agriculture Organization of the United Nations, there are some 172+ breeds of donkey worldwide - most of which are very rare and region-specific, and a few breeds thought to be extinct.

While there are a variety of donkeys, the most commonly-owned breeds of donkey are the Grand Noir du Berry, the hinny, the mule, the Poitou, and the miniature, which will get its own subsection below. Let's look at each of these common breeds in turn.

Grand Noir du Berry

This donkey breed takes its name from the Berry region of France from which it originates. The males are generally around 135-145 cm at the withers (the tallest portion of the donkey between the shoulder blades) and females around 130 cm. As the name implies, their coats are typically black but can be other colors like bay brown, dark bay brown, or grey.

This breed of donkey often has a grey belly, muzzle, thighs, and portions of their leg. They do not have the typical cross that many people associated with donkeys and also have no stripes present on the legs. Grand Noirs have a great temperament and are incredibly strong for their size.

Early on, they were found to be more useful than other animals in working with grapevines and were thus the primary animal used for this type of agriculture in the region. Their size makes it easier for them to travel between the narrow rows of vines better than horses. In the 19th century, the donkey replaced human power for pulling barges down the Berry Canal and, once approaching Paris, their usual destination, the Briare Canal.

The Grand Noir has been standardized as a breed by local organizations that promote their breeding and use. They have great temperaments and are often chosen as companion animals or pets. To this day, the Grand Noir is still used by small-scale farmers and to carry tourist packs while hiking in the region.

Hinny

A hinny is a cross-breed between a female donkey and a male horse. They most often have the external features (for example, facial features) of a horse, but the body type and size of a donkey. This is a smaller and rarer breed than a lot of the others, and it can often be confused with a mule. This breed is also genetically rare. Horses have 64 chromosomes, and donkeys have 62; the hinny has 63.

The coat color and pattern can vary widely among hinnies. The coat and type of pattern the hinny will have depend highly on the coat and markings of the parents, more so than with other breeds of the donkey.

Intact male hinnies are known to be very aggressive, and extreme caution should be used when interacting with them. They also should not be kept around livestock or other animals. You should choose a gelded male to avoid potential problems.

Mules

We won't spend much time talking about the mule in this section as we dedicate an entire chapter to them below. This breed is very common in America and is much more common there than in Europe and elsewhere.

The mule is a mix between a male donkey and a female horse.

Poitou

This is another donkey breed that takes its name from the region in which it originated, in this case, Poitou, France. The Poitou is one of the larger breeds of donkey and is distinguished by its size and its unique thick, often tangled coat.

Adult males are called *baudet* and range from around 142-153 cm in height, though they can be bigger. Females are called *anesse* and are usually about a hand (about 4 inches) shorter, and their coats don't tend to be as thick.

In earlier times, this was a breed commonly used for the breeding of mules, and their genes traversed the planet through this process. Now, they are less commonly used to breed mules, like any breed of donkey is suitable, and their population went on the decline. There wasn't much of a demand for purebred Poitous, so there was a tremendous drop in their population, and they went into a significant decline in the 1950s.

Worried that the Poitou might go extinct, studies were commissioned in the 1970s, and they showed that females were having fewer pregnancies and also fewer pregnancies that were able to come to term. This led to the launch of the Save the Baudet (SABAUD) movement, which continues to this day. This organization was launched in an effort to keep the animal from going extinct and finding ways to boost their population numbers.

Stud books have been opened, and information is shared to help encourage the breeding and continued existence of the Poitou breed of donkey. Experimental breeding programs have also been set up to find more effective ways for successful breeding. Though the process is slow-going and arduous, the population climbed again in the mid-90s, and the effort is ongoing.

Miniature Donkeys

Also called a Miniature Mediterranean Donkey, this is a totally separate breed from what are considered standard donkeys. They originate from the islands of Sardinia and Sicily.

For the animal to truly be considered miniature, it cannot be any taller than 91 cm at the withers. Their parentage will also need to be documented as a miniature for them to be officially considered part of this breed.

These are uncommonly small and sweet animals and are one of the most well-known breeds of donkey for their cuteness. They come in a wide variety of different colored patterns and may or may not have markings. They range between black, grey, brown, cream, chestnut, spotted, and skewbald (animals with patches of white and another color, but typically not black).

The history of these animals is interesting. As they are so small, peasants found them very useful for turning grinding stones inside the home to grind grain. They became so well known for this use that in the 18th century, this task took on more industrial proportions. The animals were used in large scale grain mills and would be blindfolded, left to turn circles for hour after hour, grinding massive quantities of grain. Thankfully, they rarely serve this function anymore, especially not in an industrial capacity.

As with other breeds of donkey, they can also be used for small scale agricultural work. They also proved especially useful at carrying water and other supplies through mountainous or otherwise inhospitable regions. Today, they are most commonly kept as pets since they are known for gentle and sweet temperament, and their size is more conducive to being a pet.

Chapter 3: Purchasing Your Donkeys: Selection, Cost, and Other Tips

The actual purchasing of donkeys might seem like the easiest part of the ownership process, but it actually comes with a ton of important considerations. These animals require special care and are long-lived, which shows why it is so important to carefully consider a variety of aspects before buying a donkey. Some important steps in the buying process can help to ensure that you make a good decision and investment with your money.

Considerations to Address When Buying Donkeys

It takes a bit of research and some due diligence to ensure that you get animals that suit your specific needs and abilities. This isn't like making an impulse purchase of something that doesn't matter; donkeys are living creatures with emotional and physical needs that you will be responsible for providing it with. You must clearly understand what is involved with owning and raising donkeys for any purpose, but also the specific purpose with which you intend to use them.

There isn't really a pet store where you can go buy a donkey, so you will need to do some homework, and what follows are tips as to how to look for the right donkey for your needs. You will need to do a lot of legwork, but these animals are an investment, and a long-term one, so it just makes plain sense to ensure that you know what you are getting into and that you get a healthy animal that is trained or well-suited for your intended uses.

First, A Warning About Buying Online

Just like with most things today, you can look at and purchase donkeys online, but you should use a lot of caution when doing this and it is not advised that you purchase animals online, without having physically seen them first. As great as the internet is, it is also a place where scams and shady people run rampant. It is far too easy to make a professional-looking website and grab pictures of healthy, happy animals from elsewhere on the web and use them as your own.

Customer testimonials can also be faked and easily bought online. This is why it is imperative that if you are looking at donkeys online, you do that extra homework to make sure that the breeder or vendor is actually legit and who they say they are. You can make successful purchases of animals online, and many people do because of the convenience, but you shouldn't shop for and buy animals online, sight unseen. Never ever deal with someone who is reluctant or simply refuses to let you see the animals in person before purchasing. This is a huge red flag that the operation is not legit and that you may either get scammed out of your money or end up with an unhealthy or ill-tempered animal for which you will then spend time (and often, money) figuring out what to do with.

The internet can be a good starting point when shopping. It can be a great source of information for anything you need to know about donkeys and their care, but it is not the ideal place to carry out the entire purchasing process as there is a lot you need to see in person when deciding on which animal or animals to buy.

General Considerations

As we briefly touched on in the introduction, some homework is required in determining what kind of donkey to purchase and where to purchase it from. You need to consider your expectations, your skill and knowledge level, the amount of space you have available. There are resources involved with the long-term ownership and care of donkeys, and you should be able to manage these and not just the initial purchase. You can make money raising and using donkeys for specific activities, but it still requires regular inputs, training, medical care, and so on.

Remember, donkeys often live into their 30s and beyond. It isn't like buying a fish; it is a long-term investment and commitment. You need to be able to commit to decades of care and ownership.

Unless you are keeping the donkey as a pet, and sometimes even in that case, you will want your donkey to have other donkeys for companions. They are incredibly social animals and rarely fare well and have a lot of emotional distress without contact with other equines.

Consider the space you have to dedicate to the donkeys. You might look around and think you have plenty of space for 'x' number of donkeys, but they need to have plenty of room to run and have adequate space for browsing. Each animal will need at least half an acre for browsing, so you will need to plan the size of your brood.

Since we can get flustered when put on the spot, have a list of questions prepared in advance, so you don't forget to ask all pertinent questions of the breeder or vendor. Know what type of animal (breed, temperament, or training, etc.) you are looking for, so the breeder has the information they need to help you choose the best animals. When you have narrowed down your selection, ask to see the animals in a variety of settings. Ask to see them in the stables, in the pasture, being groomed, and ask to see their feet to ensure their hooves are well-trimmed and in good repair.

You mustn't make an emotional purpose because you think an animal is cute or sweet. You want the animals for a specific purpose, and you want to make sure that you choose an animal-based on those needs and desires. It's easy to get caught up in the sweet eyes of an affectionate donkey, but if that personality or skill set doesn't serve the purposes you are getting the animal for in the first place, it won't be a good fit. This isn't something you want to have buyer's remorse over.

Physically Go See the Donkeys for Yourself

Whether you scope out a potential breeder or vendor online or you simply connect with someone local, it is vital that you physically go out and see the animals so you can make sure you are getting what you are being told you are getting. Though there are plenty of great, knowledgeable, and reputable donkey breeders, there are also people just looking to make a quick buck. They perhaps don't know what they are doing or simply cut corners to save on costs, which can lead you to be saddled with a subpar or unhealthy animal.

When possible, take someone with you with in-depth knowledge and lots of experience with donkeys. They will know what to look for, questions to ask that you might not have thought of, and red flags that may indicate that things are not what they seem.

Especially when buying a purebred or miniature donkey, you want to make sure that you are actually getting what you think you are getting. Purebreds and miniatures come at a higher price tag than other donkeys, so you want to make sure you are actually getting an official, legitimate breed.

By going to look at the animals, not only can you be sure that you are getting the breed you wanted, you can see the conditions the animal is kept in. You want animals that are kept in clean, healthy, and safe conditions, so they don't come to you sick or stressed out.

Setting up an appointment for viewing is imperative, but experts recommend you visit more than once.

If at all possible, show up unexpectedly on your second visit, so you know they haven't created a fake or idealized environment simply for your behalf. You want to know what the actual conditions the animal is kept in are like.

In addition, to make sure you are getting the breed you expect and that the animals are in good condition physically, you also want to make sure that you are getting an animal with the right temperament and/or training for your desired needs. You will be looking for quite different things when looking for a donkey to be a pet as opposed to a donkey used to guard livestock. Clearly understand your expectations and needs when deciding which breeds or specific animals will be best suited for you.

For example, if you want a donkey that will be good for young children learning to ride, you don't want a fresh, untrained animal. It takes a lot of skill, experience, and years of training to prepare a donkey to accept and tolerate being ridden in order for it to be safe for children to ride them. Don't take the breeders word for it; it is always better to demand evidence and be sure.

If the breeder or vendor tells you the animal has been handled or trained, request a proof. Ask to see the animal interact with people and being ridden so you know that you are getting an animal that will be safe for your children to ride on.

A Note on Males

Intact males are well known for being quite aggressive and difficult to handle and train. They can be unpredictable and may be dangerous for people who lack experience. Most experts recommend getting gelded males unless you plan on breeding them. Even if you plan on breeding them, you will need to keep the intact male away from other animals and use extreme caution when handling them for care. It is best to get a gelded male or make sure that you have the costs of castration included in your purchasing figures.

Gelding can be a complicated process that involves someone with experience and specialty, and it's expensive to have a male gelded after purchase. Many breeders and vendors will have already gelded males for sale, and choosing these is recommended.

A Note on Miniatures

We should also touch on the particulars of purchasing miniature donkeys. Since this is a specialty breed, they typically command a price higher than other donkeys, even some purebred varieties. The animal, as we noted above, must meet certain criteria to be officially a miniature and thus command the higher price tag. If you are in the market for a miniature donkey, make sure the breeder can provide you with proof of age and parentage.

Though it isn't all that common, people have tried to pass off smaller donkeys or even ailing, malnourished older donkeys, like miniatures, so you want to have the proof for the peace of mind it provides.

Cost

Since any animal will require regular and ongoing care, you will want to know all the costs involved not only in the purchase of the animals but their care. You will need to budget for hay, water, protection from the elements, trace mineral salt supplements, drenching, and regular hoof trimming. To keep donkeys healthy, annual vaccinations for things like influenza are recommended. Breeding animals will come with a whole range of costs too detailed for this kind of basic overview.

Typically, depending on the breed, age, and training of the animals, donkeys will range in price from around $500-2,000.

After choosing your animals and making the purchase, ask for a written receipt with as much pertinent information as possible documented on it. The receipt should include the following information:

- Vendor's name
- Vendor's address
- Vendor's phone number and email address (if applicable)
- Date of sale
- Cost of sale
- Any additional information such as the inclusion of tack or transport

Equine Passports

To legally purchase a donkey, you will need to have a certificate of sale and an equine passport. All donkeys should come with an equine passport, or it will not be a legally-recognized purchase. First, you want to confirm before visiting that all their animals have legitimate equine passports. You will also want to ask to see the document before you finalize the purchase.

Since there is a legal element to this, you will want to make sure all your proverbial ducks are in a row. It isn't enough just to have the breeder's word that all the animals have an equine passport; you will want to see the document and make sure it is official.

When shown the passport, you will want to verify that the breeder or vendor information is correct and what you were given when working with them. You may also consider checking with the issuer of the passports to make sure that they are valid. If you don't have the certificate of sale and equine passport, not only can you end up being fined in certain areas, you will have no legal recourse if there is a problem.

Once you have done your homework, made a visit or two, and chosen your animals, it is time to make the purchase final and decide how you will get the animals home. Some breeders and vendors will include transport in the cost of the animal; others expect you to find your own transportation, which will involve the use of a trailer and a truck suitable for pulling an animal trailer.

If the cost of transport is included in your purchase, ask to see the trailer the animals are being transported in. You want to make sure that it is in good repair and a safe space for the animals to travel in. You don't want to have too many animals in one trailer where they may be unsafe, uncomfortable, and overstressed. That doesn't start the animal off on a particularly good footing at their new home. It is best if there can be as little stress as possible, which, of course, isn't easy, especially if the animals have to endure long-distance travel to get to their new home.

If you are responsible for their transport, you will either need to own or otherwise obtain access to a truck suitable for hauling an animal trailer. You will then need a trailer adequately sized for the number of animals you intend to transport. You will need to make sure the animals are properly protected and secured in the trailer, so you don't risk injury during the journey from one place to another.

Chapter 4: Housing Your Donkeys

While donkeys are hardy animals, they evolved in warmer climates that don't get a ton of rain, may have unstable terrain, and often have very nutrient-poor forage to eat. This is the climate across large swaths of the world, but in places like the United States and Europe, the climate can be much different, with long periods of cold and, sometimes, a lot of rain. As we noted in an earlier section, donkeys do not have an undercoat as horses have, so they have no protection from the rain or cold weather and cannot tolerate being left exposed to either for long.

Basic shelter is necessary for any place that sees regular rain or has winter. The shelter need not be huge or anything extremely complicated either. Simple structures made from basic materials will work just fine. You just have to make sure that the animals have the correct space, adequate protection from the elements, and a safe environment to seek protection from the elements.

You don't have to be a builder or a professional carpenter to build a simple shelter. With just a basic understanding of how to use basic tools and the right supplies and you can put together a nice shelter that will keep your animals safe, even in harsh conditions. Below are some basic instructions on how to build a simple shelter for your donkeys. You may need to research some of the terms if you are unfamiliar with them, but we use a simple language as possible to explain the steps needed to build a shelter.

A plan and a trip to your local hardware store are all you need to get started. That, and some good old hard work, because building a shelter, even a simple one, is hard work. Most people, even those with rudimentary building skills, can put together a simple shelter in just a few days. If you are building an enclosure for just a couple of animals, you can likely get the project complete over a weekend if you have a bit of help.

How to Build a Basic Donkey Shelter

You want to create a safe and comfortable enclosure for your animals that provides them with the amount of space and things they need to stay safe from the elements. You will want to make sure that your shelter is large enough for your animals. Most of the time, donkeys prefer to be outside, so they will likely spend most of their time outside of the enclosure, but you will want to make sure there is enough room should all the animals need to seek shelter simultaneously.

If you just have a couple of animals, an 8' x 8' enclosure will suffice. If you have many animals, you will want to make sure that you are providing adequate space for the animals. Most experts recommend giving about 40 sq. ft. of space per animal.

The basic instructions we use in this guide use the assumption that only donkeys will be kept in the enclosure. You will want to find more specific guidelines if you are looking to house your donkeys with other equines or other animals as their needs are a bit different. It will require more complicated planning to keep all the animals safe while still providing for their individual needs.

When deciding on a plan for your shelter, consider your landscape and the weather in your area. This will determine what you will need to include in your designs.

Once you have decided how large you want the structure to be, you will want to write out a simple plan with the appropriate measurements for your enclosure. The size of the space will not only depend on the number of animals you have but the open space you have available on your property.

Having a good plan will make it much easier to find what you need at the hardware store, so you don't get stuck making multiple trips because you keep forgetting something. You will need tools like a mason line, hammers, nails, and screws; a power drill can be very helpful. For the building itself, you will need:

- Properly-sized wooden poles for a frame

- Properly-sized lengths of wood to build the sidewall frame

- Wood for the roof

- Joist holders

- Shingles

- Glue for shingles

- Nails or screws

- Concrete (optional, some build wood floors since they are easier on the hooves)

- Framing for the door

- Chipboard or sheets of wood to line the framed walls and seal up the enclosure

To start, you will need a foundation. It is best if the foundation of the shelter is as level with the surrounding ground as possible. You will likely want to dig out the foundation so that after the wood or concrete is laid, it will be mostly flush with the ground. The foundation is one of the most important elements of the shelter, and great care needs to be taken to make sure the structure is on a level base.

Most people measure out their foundation using a mason's line as it is a simple and effective way of creating an evenly-sized space. Some people use concrete in the foundation, but this can be rough on the hooves of the donkey, so it should be lined with earth or hay. Others will make a wooden floor (be careful there isn't enough space between the boards for a hoof to get caught), while others just simply leave the floor earthen. It just depends on your land and your preferences; you just want to make sure they aren't standing for extended periods of time on hard and rough surfaces.

After you have your foundation built, it is time to make a pole frame for the building itself. Pole frame buildings are simpler to build than any other style, and they are known for being very sturdy and durable. They are also cheaper to construct than many other types of buildings. Especially if you don't have a ton of building skills, this is the building for you.

A pole frame consists of thick, sturdy, upright wooden posts that will bear the weight of the structure and thus need to be firmly rooted in the ground. It is recommended that your posts be placed around 2 feet (24 inches) in the ground to give them the strength they need to hold the roof on solidly.

Most woods made for outdoor use has been treated, and donkeys chew on pretty much anything, but wood especially. You will want to make sure that you restrict access to any treated wood to ensure that the donkey doesn't get sick.

After you have your major load-bearing uprights in place, you will use horizontal wooden lengths to frame the rest of the shelter around its perimeter. This will finish out the basic framing of the enclosure and will be where you attach walls and/or siding to the outside of the shelter. This step comes after the roof supports and joists are in place.

So, naturally, next, we come to roof supports. To keep the roof upright and stable, you will need roof joists. You will want to install joist supporters along the top edge of your wood frame in the spots where you will be putting wooden joists. Once the supports are in place, you can install the wooden joists.

When building the roof, you need to consider the amount of snow that you regularly receive and ensure that the roof can bear that amount of weight. If you aren't sure that it can bear the weight, you may have to come out and regularly clear the snow off the roof, which can be a real hassle.

Once your roof boards and materials are laid, shingle the roof as this will help to protect the wood from rotting, and from excessive expansion and contraction with changes in temperature.

Before you begin to shore up the sides and inside of the structure, you will want to consider the door. Some people have a typical stable door in their shelters. This is fine, but you want to make sure that the door is tall enough that the donkey can't jump over it and short enough that they can see over it. Some people simply don't have a door, which gives the donkey free reign to come in and out as they please. If you choose not to have a door, consider the most common direction the wind comes from and face the door away from the wind as best as possible.

A lot of longtime donkey owners claim that their animals prefer the open style rather than having a traditional stable door, but it just depends on the animals and the preferences of the owner. Since donkeys typically prefer to be outside in natural settings, it can be easier not to have a door and allow them to choose whether they want to be inside or not. However, the stable door will give you control over when they are in the shelter or outside. Again, it just depends on what you prefer. The ideal size for a door for the donkey enclosure measures 4' x 3'6".

Once this decision has been made, you will want to put up your outside walls. You can use weather-treated boards if you wish to keep the entire structure in a simple slat board style, or you can line outside walls with siding of your choice. One thing to note is that no treated wood should be accessible to your animals as they chew on wood. Many veterinarians argue that treated wood can make animals ill.

You will need to shore up the inside of the structure to keep your animals away from treated wood and to have a place to attach food and water holders. Many people just line the inside of the structure with chipboard sheets to provide a more finished look and to keep the animals from chewing the treated boards and posts.

Ventilation and airflow are also important, so some people leave a little clearance between the foundation and the walls of the structure to allow air to flow more easily through the shelter. You can also leave a bit of space between boards in the walls if you choose not to side the building, but you want to make sure that it isn't wide enough for an animal to get their hoof caught between boards.

Some use exhaust fans with locking shutters as a means of ventilation, and this is an excellent choice, especially if you are keeping a larger number of animals. Humidity can quickly get out of hand in a poorly-ventilated enclosure, which can make the animals sick.

Other Shelter Elements

In the wild, donkeys graze with their heads down, so eating from the ground is their natural means of eating. A floor-level feeder for supplemental hay is a great way to provide the animals with forage while still using their natural mode of consumption. The Donkey Sanctuary recommends a feeding trough that measures approximately 2' wide by 3' x 2'3" deep.

Your animals will always need easy access to forage in the winter and clean water.

We briefly noted earlier that many would line the floor of the shelter with some sort of bedding. It is important that clean straw is used and that the material is water-resistant or is frequently changed. Donkeys can become ill if left with a rotting or overly-moist straw, so it is vital to clean the enclosure regularly and to replace the straw; otherwise, the animals may become ill.

Some people will use wood shavings as bedding, but most agree that straw is the best choice. There are products that you can buy that will help reduce moisture, such as Stall Dry or Sweet PD2.

Lighting may also be a consideration. Since most donkey shelters have one side open, this isn't often a problem, but in certain areas or with certain types of enclosure, it can get pretty dark in these enclosures, and donkeys don't like to be kept in the dark. If so, you will want to provide some supplemental lighting. Make sure that all cords are kept out of reach of the animals, and guards are installed on any lights that they can reach.

Winter Donkey Care

Before we dive into winter donkey care, we should make a note about shelters in the summer. Though donkeys prefer to stay out in the open, they may seek shelter on days that are incredibly hot and sunny to avoid dehydration or heat exhaustion. They should have access to shelter year-round and always have ready access to clean water. If you choose to use misting fans, make sure that all cords are secure and out of the donkey's reach because they will try to chew on them.

Some people will put misting fans in the shelter during the summer to help keep their animals cool or will hose donkeys down with water on particularly hot days. If you use either option in the shelter, remember that this will cause the bedding to become moist. This can then cause bacteria and fungus to grow, and it will need to be replaced after each misting or hosing down.

Now onto winter. If you live in a cold area, you may want to insulate the shelter to help protect the animals from intense cold and wind. If you notice any condensation in the structure, it is a sign you do not have adequate ventilation, and you will need to address this since moisture can cause a host of different issues in donkeys.

As with any season, donkeys in winter will need to be provided with adequate supplemental food and water. It isn't recommended to keep the enclosure warmer than 50 degrees. Water, naturally, is prone to freezing in the winter, so you will need to make sure that the water you leave for the donkeys doesn't get so cold it freezes and is inaccessible to the animals. Some people will use an automated water heating system to keep the water free of ice.

You will also want to supply the animal with a vitamin and mineral balancer or a mineral salt lick.

If you have only a few animals, try to keep the space suitable to that number as it will be much harder to keep an overly-large enclosure warm enough during the winter months to protect the animals.

For those who live in areas that have bitterly cold winters, donkey rugs and protective ear coverings may be necessary to ensure they are protected from the cold. If you use these, you will need to remove them daily to brush the animal and occasionally change it if it becomes soiled or wet. Older and underweight animals are most likely to need this additional protection.

It is advised to be prepared for winter by laying in a supply of supplemental hay and bedding to make sure you have what you need for the cold months ahead. Before the weather gets cold, it is a great time to make sure your animals are current on vaccinations, has their teeth looked at, and to either have a farrier come out or inspect and trim hooves yourself if you have the proper skill and tools.

Rain Scald and mud fever are two common conditions that can plague donkeys during the winter, especially if the donkey doesn't have access to a dry environment. Rain Scald typically affects the shoulder back and rump. Mud fever affects lower extremities.

Outdoor Space Considerations

Donkeys are known to wander away from their home territory, so fencing is an important element to ensure you don't have a bunch of escaping donkeys you have to track down and return. Enclosed spaces work best, and typically most pasture is fenced in. Wood makes good fencing, but as we have mentioned numerous times, donkeys are likely to chew on the material, so if you use wood, it will occasionally need to be replaced or repaired. The fence should be at least 4' tall, so the donkeys cannot jump it.

Regular inspections are recommended to ensure your fence stays in good repair, especially if it is made from wood.

You will need to consider the type of vegetation on your land as there are plants that are known to be toxic to donkeys. Remove any poisonous plants from their pasture area, or keep the animals from accessing this area. Your local agriculture department can tell you if any poisonous native plants should be removed from your property before letting donkeys graze.

You should not graze donkeys on alfalfa grass as it is rich food, and donkeys are evolved to survive on nutrient-poor forage. Alfalfa is remarkably high in certain nutrients that donkeys aren't used to consuming in such quantities, and this can lead to stomach upset or other gastrointestinal issues.

Donkeys, as we have mentioned a couple of times, cannot have sudden changes in their food source. This will lead to gastrointestinal issues. Any new food or forage will need to be introduced slowly, usually over a couple of weeks, to allow them to adjust to the new food source.

You will need to provide numerous places to access clean water, and if your pastureland is large, you will want to place water troughs in various places around the property.

Mud is something that you will also want to keep an eye out for. Donkeys left standing in muddy areas can develop a range of different foot issues, so they should spend most of their time on dry ground.

Many people will use de-icers or other salt-based products to keep down on the ice during the winter, but this use is not recommended around donkeys. Salt will accumulate on surfaces, and this can cause problems with their hooves.

If your animals are getting the bulk of their calories from the pastureland itself and not from supplemental feeding, it is important to leave certain sections fallow. This will ensure that it can regenerate after significant grazing; otherwise, the land will quickly be exhausted and unable to support forage growth.

Chapter 5: Feeding Your Donkeys

Though donkeys are a species of equine, they have hugely different nutritional needs than horses or other equines. Due to the environment they evolved in, they are accustomed to a diet of nutrient-poor forage, and rich foods that are high in nutrients will cause colic, stomach upset, and potentially a host of other gastrointestinal issues. This is why you must keenly understand the nutritional needs of these animals so you can provide them with appropriate food for their needs.

Donkey Eating Habits

In their natural environment, donkeys are grazers. This means that they will browse a small amount of forage often throughout the day. They will consume roughly 1.3-1.8% of their body weight in forage daily. They are not used to – or meant to – eat food in large quantities. These animals will overeat, which can lead to a whole host of issues, so you will need to control their access to supplemental forage. Restricted grazing is also a means to help control the amount of food the animal eats at a given time. There are many different kinds of supplemental forage you can give to donkeys, which we will look at below. Still, the Donkey Sanctuary recommends barley straw as the best source of supplemental nutrition.

In the winter, donkeys will not likely have access to the forage and natural browsing they get in the summer, so they may largely or exclusively subsist off supplemental foods. This means you will need to provide them with a controlled amount of food daily, most often straw or a substance called haylage, which we will discuss below.

If any of your donkeys are ill or underweight, they will need extra high fiber forage, and you may want to consider supplementing their forage with vitamins.

For those with decent pasture, donkeys will require little supplemental feeding during the summer, but if your land is poor, more will be required.

As we have noted numerous times, donkeys will overeat. An overfed donkey is more prone to issues such as laminitis and hyperlipemia. These can be serious conditions and is further proof of the necessity of controlling the amount of food they have access to.

Barley straw, as we mentioned earlier, is the best source of supplemental nutrition for donkeys since it is low in sugar and high in fiber. Oat straw can be used and may actually be preferable for underweight or ill donkeys since it is higher in nutrients than barley straw. Use caution when feeding oat straw to healthy animals, as they can over-eat.

Younger animals or those with strong teeth can eat wheat straw, but it is not recommended for older animals or those with poor teeth. Wheat straw is lower in nutrition than the other types of straw we discuss here, so it isn't ideal. You will want to avoid linseed straw completely. Animals can safely eat the straw, the seeds are poisonous, and it is almost impossible to ensure that there are no seeds in linseed straw. It can be boiled to help reduce the toxicity of the seeds, but again, it can still cause issues that lead many to avoid this straw type entirely.

Hay can also be used as a food supplement besides being a great source for bedding for a donkey enclosure. Like straw, different types of hay are more or less suitable for donkeys. Make sure that any hay used for feeding or bedding is free of moisture and fungal growth.

What follows are the most common types of hay:

- Meadow hay - this comprises a mix of natural grasses and is safe to use for feed.

- Seed hay - this is usually made from rye or timothy and refers to the stems that are left after the seeds have been collected. It is also suitable for use as a supplemental feed.

- Hay from cow pastures - since this hay tends to be rich in nutrients, it isn't the best source of supplemental food for donkeys.

Ragwort can be found in many different types of hay, and it is poisonous to equine. This is why you must have a trusted and quality source of hay.

Many people grow their own hay since it isn't too difficult and can make more financial sense than buying it from a third party. Most often, hay crops are harvested between late May through July. Though it can be harvested later, the later you harvest, the lower the nutritional value of the hay will be. Once the hay is harvested, it will need to be kept in a dry, well-ventilated space for at least three months.

Freshly-cut hay shouldn't be offered to donkeys as it can cause stomach upset like colic. Hay is considered ready for use when it reaches 85% dryness.

Haylage is another source of supplemental food sometimes given to donkeys for feed. Haylage is partially-wilted grass that has been dried, but not to the level that hay is dried. Typically, haylage is about 55-65% dry. To make haylage, once the grass is baled, you will want to seal it with strong plastic that is free from tears. If there are any tears in the plastic, dangerous mold can develop in just a few days, ruining the crop for use with donkeys and most other livestock animals.

Never feed donkeys silage (grass or other green fodder compacted and stored in airtight conditions, typically in a silo, without first being dried, and used as animal feed in the winter) as it has a much too high level of moisture and is far too low in fiber to make proper food for these animals.

If you don't have a good source of hay or haylage, high fiber pellets are another way to supplement your donkey's diet. It may also be preferable for use with animals with laminitis or need to put on weight. Since they are so much higher in nutrition than natural forage or hay, you will want to give the animals small amounts at a time, so they don't overeat.

If you are feeding a donkey with bad teeth, soaking the pellets in water will soften them and make them easier to eat. You will want to avoid pellets from mixed sources as they may be high in cereal grains, which aren't good for donkeys and do not provide their ideal nutrition.

Now, let's consider a substance called *chaff*, which can be used as a supplemental food source. Chaff is a mixture of chopped hay and straw and often has oils or other supplemental vitamins and minerals added to it. Animals with bad teeth or that struggle to eat straw may find this a preferable food source that is easier for them to manage. It is also a good choice in supplemental feed for donkeys that suffer from laminitis.

Chaff should have a sugar content of less than 8% and will often be listed as laminitic safe on the packaging.

Old or sick donkeys may benefit from supplemental feeding of small amounts of dried sugar beet pulp, which is a byproduct of the sugar production process. This is not a replacement for hay or other supplemental food but is an excellent source of fiber and is more nutritious than hay or straw.

Sugar beet pulp tends to come in shreds and should not be given to the animals straight. It needs to be soaked before it is safe to give to your donkeys. Most often, it will need to be soaked for about 24-hours, but there are now varieties that offer a quick soak method. Some modern, quick soak varieties can be ready to eat in as little as ten minutes. The proper means of soaking will be listed on the manufacturer's instructions.

Additional Food for Donkeys

Some people will give their animals a few fruits and vegetables as a supplement for their diet. Not only is this a great way to give the animals some variety, but it is also known to help spurn appetite in animals that may be struggling to eat. Fruits and vegetables are often given in winter but make an appropriate treatment at any time of year. Late winter and early spring are "lean times" for sources of hay and other supplemental forage, making this a good way to keep the animals healthy and full, even if hay or straw isn't readily available.

You shouldn't give animals any stone fruits (fruits with a large seed in the middle), potatoes, garlic, or any type of spoiled produce. Donkeys enjoy things like carrots, apples, bananas, pears, and turnips. The produce should be cut into small chunks to make it easier for the donkey to manage.

A Note On Vitamins and Minerals

If your animals subsist entirely or largely on natural pasture, it is possible that they aren't getting all the vitamins and nutrients they need for optimal health. Vitamin and mineral supplements often called *balancers*, are a great means of providing any nutrients they may lack their daily diet.

Some people prefer to use mineralized blocks to provide needed supplemental vitamins and nutrients but is it vital that you don't get a mineral block intended for horses. Horses have quite different nutritional requirements, and these blocks may contain substances that are toxic or unsuitable for donkeys. There are mineral blocks made especially for donkeys, which is used if this is the form of vitamin and mineral supplementation you choose.

For animals that need to lose weight or maintain their current body weight, there are several supplements recommended by the Donkey Sanctuary for this purpose. TopSpec Donkey Forage Balancer is highly recommended. If you are dealing with pregnant, older, or ill animals, products like TopSpec Comprehensive Balancer are a great choice.

Final Thoughts On Feeding

The following should be adhered to for feeding your donkeys:

- All food should be free of mold and fungus

- Feed the animals the proper foods for their nutritional needs

- Feed the animals small amounts, regularly, and control the amount of food they have access to.

- Any dietary changes should be made slowly, over time, typically over a period of 7-14 days.

- Avoid foods high in sugar.

- Make sure nutritional supplements are suitable for donkeys and readily available.

- Never feed your donkeys grass clippings.

We have stressed several times and will stress again, that while donkeys are equine, they are not horses. They have quite different needs, and requirements and some things that are safe and suitable for horses are not so for donkeys. Never assume that something meant for horses is okay to use on a donkey. For example, horses eat nutrient-rich feed which, if given to donkeys, is likely to cause colic or a range of other gastrointestinal issues.

Vitamin supplements for horses are also not suitable for donkeys as they often contain nutrients at higher levels than are suitable for donkeys and may contain substances harmful to them.

Part of their physical adaptation to their environment, and what makes them so popular in harsh climates, is their ability to subsist on sparse, low-nutrient foods, quite different from what a horse needs. It takes donkeys longer to digest their food than other animals, including horses, as this allows them to derive as much nutritional value from their food as possible.

Donkeys, unlike ponies and horses, can recycle nitrogen, which is a unique adaptation to a low nutrient environment. In horses, nitrogen is expelled as urea by the kidneys and released from the body via urine. Donkeys can reabsorb the urea, which allows them to reuse the nitrogen. This process is naturally regulated in response to the amount of nitrogen available in their food supply, and how much protein they are getting.

Crude protein requirements are much less for donkeys than they are for horses. A donkey only needs a daily intake of about 3.8-7.4% crude protein, whereas a horse requires between 8-12%. This figure alone shows that what is good for a horse may well not be for a donkey and vice versa.

Donkeys will browse on more than just grass, which can become a frustration for people with a lot of trees or shrubs on their pasture. Donkeys eat trees, shrubs, flowering plants, and well, pretty much any vegetation that may be growing on your land. If forage is limited, but other types of plant material are not, a donkey can quickly destroy the other vegetation.

Some people provide brambles or shrubs intended for the donkey to browse on to try to keep them from destroying surrounding trees or other desirable vegetation and can be an effective deterrent.

Overall, with a donkey's diet, foods high in fiber and low in sugar are most important. Some animals get the bulk of their nutrition from browsing and need truly little supplementation in their diet. Others that are housed on grounds with poor forage or pasture may rely largely or even entirely on straw or other forms of supplemental foods.

Pasture is ideal as it is more akin to their natural environment. It allows them to graze slowly and makes them less prone to overeating than animals fed largely on supplemental hay or straw. Animals on pasture also get more exercise, and this is vital to keeping them healthy and maintaining a healthy weight. Whether they are fed exclusively on hay or straw, forage, or a combination of the two, provide the appropriate amount of supplemental vitamins and minerals to ensure they get a fully balanced diet that meets all their nutritional requirements.

It is incredibly important, hence why we repeat it, to understand that donkeys have evolved to consume foods low in nutritional content. Their digestive systems are even designed for this purpose, allowing them to get every possible amount of nutrition from the poor-quality forage they consume. This can be a concern for land that has been improved as it may grow higher quality pasture than donkeys are accustomed to consuming.

If your property has forage that is too high in nutritional value for the donkeys, one way to accommodate the animals is to let the grass go to seed before allowing the donkeys to feed on it. This lowers the nutritional quality of the grasses, which makes it easier for the animals to digest properly. You may also want to consider sowing the land with lower nutrient grasses that are more suitable to the needs of donkeys.

Chapter 6: Training Your Donkeys

Donkeys are known for being stubborn, but this isn't the fairest criticism. Donkeys are cautious animals that like to think about what they do before they do it. This means it can take them longer to learn certain behaviors or skills, but it shouldn't be seen as the animal being obstinate. They need time to understand what you are asking them to do and how to do it. Yet, while it may take them a little longer to pick up on a skill or behavior, they are more likely to remember and retain it than a horse. Basically, this means that you won't have to keep working with the donkey on the same skill for as long as you would a horse.

Understanding how your donkeys learn will better help you to develop a training routine that makes sense for the animal you are training and is more likely to succeed.

Different types of training will be employed depending on what you plan to use the animals for. It is best to start with some general or basic training and then move on to more difficult moves and maneuvers.

Basic Training

Though it isn't always possible, it is best to train donkeys as foals. The earlier training can begin, the easier it is to develop the bond with them that is needed for them to follow your orders and perform certain tasks. You want to imprint on the foal. This means they learn your physical presence, smell, sound, and touch when it is possible to do so. The earlier a bond can be developed, the easier it is to train your donkey later.

Sometimes, though, the jenny isn't entirely comfortable with someone coming in and handling her foal. If so, you may need to socialize the jenny before you can approach the foal. She needs to be comfortable enough with you that she will let you near her foal without causing her undue stress or making her aggressive.

Even if you aren't starting out with a foal, socialization is an important part of any training routine. The animal needs to trust you, and you both need to know each other well enough to take verbal and nonverbal cues from each other. The more time you spend with the animals, the better the bond will become. The process for socialization - spending time with the animal, letting them get used to your scent, talking to the animal, and handling the animal - will be the same, whether you are working with a foal or an adult animal. Just know the older the animal is, the longer it may take to socialize them.

There are several ways that people train donkeys, but the most effective way is through positive reinforcement. This reinforcement utilizes positive rewards as opposed to negative actions or punishment. Different types of reinforcement have long been studied, and science has shown this is one of the most effective means of teaching donkeys new skills. They respond far better to rewards than the removal of something unpleasant (like in negative reinforcement) or punishment.

All donkeys are unique creatures and learn in slightly different ways, so while positive reinforcement is the most commonly used and most effective way to train donkeys, with certain animals, a different mode of reinforcement may be necessary.

With positive reinforcement, you are essentially offering the animal a reward for following command or request. The animal is more likely to perform if they know the result is getting something they like.

Most often, treats, sometimes paired with a clicker, are used as the reward in a positive reinforcement schedule. While food works best, some animals will respond well to physical praise and thus may not require the treats to learn certain skills. You are likely to get better results if you go the treat route.

Positive reinforcement has numerous benefits. Besides it being a proven and effective way to teach an animal new skills, it will also help to strengthen your bond with the animal, which will help in later training.

Before we move on to specific modes of training, let's take a quick look at the other types of reinforcement that may be employed in donkey training.

Negative Reinforcement

This type of reinforcement is often called the Natural Horsemanship process and seeks to train animals using their basic natural instincts and modes of communication. Pain is not used in this type of reinforcement, but discomfort is. For example, unpleasant pressure may be used, followed by the release of said pressure when the animal performs the desired task.

This, as it's the alternative name implies, works decently with horses who are well known to perform a task to get relief from unpleasant pressure. It has less success with donkeys, but you may run into certain animals that will best respond to this mode of reinforcement. Horses do better with nonverbal communication than donkeys do, so donkeys are not as likely to respond well to this as a horse would be.

Extinction

We won't spend long on this reinforcement schedule as it isn't recommended for use with donkeys. The basic idea is to extinguish an undesired behavior through the removal of a particular stimulus.

Punishment

This is the least effective means of training and donkey, and many avoid it because it can be considered cruel. As the name of this schedule implies, punishment entails the introduction of something unpleasant if the animal fails to perform the desired behavior. Most people avoid this type of reinforcement with all equine, but especially donkeys, where having a close, positive bond with their trainer is so vital to the success of training efforts.

These training schedules and the means of teaching donkeys that follow rely on both main types of animal conditioning: classical conditioning and operant conditioning. Classical conditioning involves animals learning to make associations between a particular stimulus and its response. Operant conditioning relies more on trial and error. The animal learns that behavior "x" is followed by the response "y," and through this will learn the most effective means of achieving the desired result.

Regardless of the type of reinforcement you employ, the reinforcement schedule is very important. Usually the reinforcement schedule will be every time the animal performs an action or every certain number of times the animal performs the action. Training tends to work better when rewards follow the completion of every task rather than intermittent reinforcement. It can be more difficult for a donkey to pick up a skill with this schedule.

We should also point out that the age, temperament, and health of the animal will have a profound effect on how training's effectiveness. The sex of the animal can also have an impact. These things will help you determine what you should be able to expect from a given animal and the best way to achieve the desired results.

As is probably understood, older animals do not learn as fast and will not pick up as much as younger animals. This doesn't mean they can't or shouldn't be trained, but this should alter what your expectations of the animal are. Jennies in heat or intact jacks will need to be handled very differently than a foal or a gelded jack.

Like humans and most other creatures, donkeys build and strengthen neural pathways as they develop a new skill. Learning something new is harder for anyone and takes longer as no path has been developed. Conversely, a skill that builds off a simpler skill the animal always knows will likely be picked up far more quickly than a completely novel behavior.

We noted earlier in this guide that donkeys don't have nearly as strong of a flight response as horses do. This means that, while it can take longer to train a donkey, it can actually be easier than training a horse, which is naturally frightened and has a strong flight response.

Before you start any training routine, you need to have a plan set out with clearly-defined goals. This will help to ensure your training sessions are more fruitful and effective. None of the experts think it is a good idea to "wing it" for training any animal, but especially donkeys.

Finally, let's discuss equipment. All donkeys are differently sized and proportioned. It is imperative that you use gear that properly fits the specific animal. Equipment meant for horses will often be too large or too heavy to use with donkeys. You must choose a saddle or bridle that fits the animal as well as possible. Though costly, if you can afford to do so, having a custom saddle or harness is a great idea.

General Verbal Commands

The most effective way to communicate with your donkey is through the use of short, clear language. This will help them understand what you are asking them to do. You can come up with your own short verbal commands, but what follows are some of the most commonly used.

- Whoa - means stop

- Stand

- Step - this is the command for the animal to start walking

- Trot - walking at a faster clip

- Back up

- Gee - a right turn

- Haw - a left turn

- Canter

- Easy - this is telling the animal to slow down

As we mentioned, you do not have to use these standard commands, and most trainers have their own ways of making commands. Whatever you choose, short, single word commands are easiest for the animal to learn and thus most effective.

Haltering and Leading

This is one of the most basic skills to teach your donkey, as this will be required for several tasks. The first step is to get the animal used to wear a halter. You can acclimate the animal to the halter by simply letting them wear it for a while, allowing them to get comfortable having something unfamiliar on their back. This may take a few days, but once the animal can wear the halter without issue, you can move on to the next step in the training process.

Once the donkey is comfortable being harnessed, you will want to train the animal to lead or walk with a rope and follow quite simple verbal commands. First, you will want to put the lead on the animal and let it get used to it as you did with the harness. Tie the lead to something like a fence. Let the animal stay there for about 10-15 minutes and then come back and take the lead off whatever it was tied to.

Give them words of encouragement and see if they move in your direction (or at all). Even if they just move a single step, give them verbal and physical praise along with a treat they enjoy. If the donkey doesn't move, tie the lead back to the support and come back again in 15 minutes and try the same process.

It can be a slow process that requires time and quite a few treats, but this is a proven and effective way to get them accustomed to leading. Each step forward is a step forward and means you are closer to moving on to more complex training. Always offer treats and praise whenever even the smallest amount of progress is made.

Call the animal when trying to get it to come to you and reward every step they take in your direction. Once you get the donkey to come all the way to you, you can take them on walks but remember to bring plenty of treats to reward their progress. It might seem like bribery, and in truth, it is; but it is also effective, *so bribery it is*!

Sometimes unfamiliar objects will startle or scare the animal, and they need to be reassured there is nothing to fear before trying to get them to move on from whatever frightened them. Console them and try to show them there is no danger in whatever the unknown object is. Communication is vital when it comes to the successful training of donkeys.

When the animal has developed some confidence and is good at being led on walks, you will want to introduce some simple obstacles such as logs or tires. This will teach the donkey how to walk around or maneuver over obstacles that may be in their way. They probably will be reluctant at first, but with coaxing and praise, they will gain confidence and move over or around these obstacles.

You will want to slowly introduce the animal to more complicated moves like backing up or turning around once the animal is comfortable and confident with obstacles. It is important that you don't try to move this process along too fast as it may not be as successful as if you display patience.

Experts at donkey training recommend about a year of this type of training before you attempt to ride or haul things with the animal. The animal needs a lot of practice, and it needs to develop a close and positive relationship with its trainer. This means that besides working on skill development, you will also develop an emotional bond with the animal, both learning the communication style of the other, which will, in turn, make it easier to teach the animal other skills.

Driving

Training gets more complex when you introduce the donkey while driving. This complexity is why you so should develop a positive relationship and effective communication with the animal before moving on to the more complex elements of training. To learn driving, the animal must learn to stand still and respond to basic verbal commands.

Donkeys learn in a variety of ways, and part of how they can be acclimated to and become comfortable with a new skill is to see other animals performing said skill. It might seem a bit strange, but this will help the donkey get used to this being a normal occurrence and shouldn't be frightened.

And the animal will also need to get used to wearing a bridle, and the best way to do this is to acclimate them to it in the same way you got them used to wear a harness - simply put the bridle on them for periods of time so they can get accustomed to wearing it. They will also need to become acclimated with the long reins used to guide the animal and a guide whip. We will note here and other places that the whip is meant to be used as a guide, not as a punishment. You don't want to hit the animal hard with the whip, even if they aren't following your commands. Use firm but gentle pressure when using the whip.

Leaving the animal's cart somewhere on your property where he regularly goes; this is a good way to get them used to seeing it and thus will make it less likely they fear it when you go to introduce it. Some people will leave the cart on their grounds somewhere and reward the donkey if they see it investigating the cart. This will help the donkey develop a positive association with the cart.

If you are new to donkey training, you should have someone with experience with you the first time you hook your donkey up to a cart. You need to make sure that it is properly hooked up, and it can be a little complicated the first time you do it. All equipment used needs to be of appropriate size for the donkey and that the cart is properly hitched to avoid injuring the animal or yourself. Often, people will bring in outside help from someone who has successfully taught donkeys to drive to get a feel for how the process works and the best course of action for training animals in this skill.

Once the animal is comfortable being hitched to a cart, acclimate it to having the cart hitched to them. If possible, take the animal on a short, leaded walk with an empty cart. When the animal is comfortable being led with an empty cart, add some weight to the cart so they can get used to pulling as well.

After you have gotten the animal comfortable with being hitched to a cart with some weight in it, you will want to begin ground training the donkey to make different maneuvers with the cart. As the animal's level of skill develops, you can introduce more complex moves such as turning and backing up while pulling the cart. These are sophisticated moves, and you shouldn't expect that the animal will learn how to do these things overnight. This process will take time to become perfect for both you and the donkey.

Riding

We have mentioned several times in this guide that donkeys are great for teaching kids how to ride. They are also suitable for older people and those with certain disabilities. They even take regular-sized adults in certain areas with difficult terrain that are tourist attractions, such as at the Grand Canyon.

The donkey should be large enough to be ridden. Miniatures are generally only recommended as proper riding animals for children, given their small stature. Both children and adults can ride most standard donkeys.

Ground driving skills are especially important for both hauling material and being ridden. It not only gets them used to follow basic commands, but they will have learned more complex moves like turning around or backing up, which can be particularly useful and necessary when being ridden.

Like with most other things we have discussed here, you will want to let the donkey become acclimated to the new equipment they will have to wear. Putting all riding equipment on the donkey and letting them wear it for short periods of time is a highly effective way to accomplish this.

Next, you will want to spend some time mounted on the animal without it walking to allow both the animal and you to get used to being on the back. Practice mounting and dismounting on both sides of the animal to help them get used to this part of the process.

Once your animal is comfortable with the equipment, being mounted, and dismounted, it is time to get the animal used to walking with someone on their back. This is best done with another person who can lead the animal on short walks (with lots of praise and treats) while you are on the animal's back.

At every step of the way, you will want to communicate with your donkey, giving them verbal cues and praise. For example, you can say "walk-on" while gently tapping the side of the donkey with your foot to get the donkey to continue walking. Any progress should be rewarded both verbally and with a treat or physical praise like petting.

Donkeys aren't good long-haul trainers. They do best in shorter sessions of about 20 minutes, performed frequently. The process of training will follow a very similar path to that of horses, with the exception that it can take a bit longer to train a donkey to be ridden than a horse.

Lifting Feet

Donkeys, like all equine, are hooved animals, and they will require regular foot care and maintenance. This means that the animal will need to let you pick up their leg so you can clean and examine their feet regularly. Most donkeys aren't fond of this at first, but with some patience, you can acclimate the animal to let you manipulate their feet.

If the animal tries to pull away while you are working on the food, don't let go, but give the animal a lot of praise, so they know not to be alarmed or scared. This will also teach the animal that trying to pull their leg away is ineffective.

You will want to start with the front legs, but we should note here you need to use extreme caution when you start this training. Donkeys that are resistant have tried to kick the person training them, which is why it's better to have a trained professional or farrier with you the first time you start this kind of training.

Over time, the animal will get accustomed to having their legs lifted, and their feet messed with.

Guard Donkeys

Though it is less well known, as we mentioned above, donkeys are very territorial and will be aggressive with anything they see as a potential threat to their area. This is why many people choose to use donkeys as guard animals over the more traditional dog. With proper socialization and training, donkeys are an incredibly effective means of protecting flocks of livestock like sheep, goats, and cows. Once the donkey has become established with the flock, they will guard almost any kind of livestock.

The more comfortable the donkey is with the flock, the more time they will spend in and among the flock, often spending much of their day grazing alongside them. If the donkey and the flock are well bonded, the donkey will spend much, if not all, of their day with the livestock. Donkeys have a natural herding instinct and rely on keen sight and sound for detecting potential threats or predators.

If an intruder is spotted, a well-bonded donkey will physically put themselves between the flock and the potential threat. They will bray loudly, which is often effective at scaring off the potential trouble source. Not only does this distress call scare off predators, but it can also alert the owner that something may be upon the property.

Should braying prove unsuccessful, the donkey has more proverbial ammunition. The animals will rear up and attack the animal with a swift kick, which will deter and sometimes even kill the predator.

Jennies and foals raised with sheep or other livestock will have a stronger bond with the livestock and thus be better protectors to the flock. Once a foal is weaned, the jenny can be removed, and the foal left with the livestock. This is the best way to bond a donkey to the livestock they are to protect.

Even if the animal is not raised with the flock, it can be successfully introduced and become bonded with the flock. This needs to be done under close supervision. First, housing the donkey near the livestock they will guard, but not with it, will help both get used to the presence of the other.

You can then move on to having the donkey in an enclosure with the flock, but this will need to be closely supervised. Remember that donkeys are very territorial and aggressive, and it isn't all that uncommon for a new donkey to see the livestock as a threat and to act accordingly. In order to keep everyone safe until you can trust the donkey understands its role in the flock, this needs to be closely monitored, and the donkey shouldn't be left alone with the flock until you are sure they are well bonded and won't attack.

Most donkeys, even those raised apart from livestock, can be successfully bonded and become good guard animals for the flock. However, remember that donkeys, like humans, have very distinct personalities, and sometimes, certain individuals just aren't well-suited to guarding livestock.

In tack, males should not be used as they are too aggressive and can behave unpredictably. Certain donkeys can become overprotective of the flock they guard and will, at times, mistake foals for threats and can injure or kill the babies. Many people remove the donkey from the pasture when the livestock give birth to allow the foals to gain some strength and size, making them less likely to be seen as a potential threat by the guard donkey.

Donkeys have a strong dislike for any and all canines, so this is something you will need to remember if you also keep dogs on your property. For the safety of the dog, it is best to keep them away from the donkey unless they were raised together. It is not unheard of for a curious family dog to get a good kick for their efforts from an unsuspecting donkey.

One donkey can guard anywhere from 100-200 animals, depending on the size and terrain of the property in question.

Benefits of Clicker Training

Many people swear by the use of clickers for training all different kinds of animals and this method has the benefit of being both effective and straightforward to learn. Using a clicker involves operant conditioning with positive reinforcement and should be performed on a regular rewards schedule.

It seems to be so effective because it pairs a consistent sound with the reward given after the performance of the desired behavior.

First, you will need to employ a little classical conditioning to get the animal to associate the sound of the clicker with getting a treat and praise. Once the animal responds to the sound of the clicker, even when distracted, the association has become ingrained. Once this happens, the operant conditioning can begin, and the sound of the clicker will be paired with a command which will be rewarded if successfully completed.

Once it seems like the donkey has developed an association between the verbal command and reward, you can stop using the clicker and stick to only verbal cues. The length of time it will take to get to this point will depend on each individual animal.

Chapter 7: Grooming and Caring for Your Donkeys

Donkeys, like any other animal, require some basic grooming and care to keep them looking and feeling their best. While known for being low maintenance, this doesn't mean that these animals are no maintenance. They require minimal regular care, most of which is related to grooming. This helps keep their coats looking their best and keeps their eyes, nose, mouth, and hooves free of debris, which can cause discomfort or health issues.

With donkey grooming, there are a few basic tools that are required, which we will touch on below, but the toolkit most people use for grooming is specialized over time, depending on the needs and preferences of the owner and the animals.

General

Donkeys need to be kept clean and their coats free of debris, which is why you should brush them regularly, every day if possible. Grooming will be especially important in the winter for donkeys that are wearing rugs to keep them warm. The hair under the rug can easily become matted and tangled, leading to discomfort and the potential for skin issues.

Brushing donkeys dry is far preferable to brushing them wet, which can irritate their skin. Donkeys aren't very fond of getting wet, of beginning with. Most donkeys actually enjoy being groomed and will appreciate the daily care. It is also a great bonding opportunity for you and the donkey, so take advantage of this.

It should be mentioned that if you have any expectations of keeping your donkeys fully clean, you will need to let that go. Even with regular brushing, donkeys get dirty, especially as they are known to roll in the dirt, and unlike horses, don't shake it off when they are done. The main goal of grooming is to keep their hair and skin free of debris and other substances that can cause sores or irritation, not to keep them looking showroom clean (though we will touch show donkeys briefly below).

Their hooves will require regular and specialized care, just as horses do. Daily, it is recommended to clean mud, dirt, and other debris from the hooves using a hoof hook, which we will discuss below. You may want to consult the chapter on training to see how to get the animal to become used to having their feet lifted and messed with.

Like other equine, donkeys' hooves grow continuously and will need to be trimmed regularly roughly every 4-8 weeks. Failure to properly care for their hooves can lead to a range of problems that can become serious. Trimming hooves is not something everyone is comfortable doing or has the tools and skill to perform. Many rely on the occasional visit by a professional farrier for this maintenance.

Every time you groom your donkeys, take a minute to look them over and check for any cuts, skin or hoof issues, injuries, or any sign of illness. Catching problems early will help reduce the likelihood that the animal will experience major problems. You will also want to consider their teeth for any signs of rot, damage, or sharp edges. Donkey's teeth are always growing, and they get worn down by the coarse forage they eat. This can lead to sharp edges on the teeth, which can then lead to mouth sores. Have your donkeys looked at if you notice any issues. You will want to have their teeth looked at professionally about once a year.

If a donkey has poor or damaged teeth, switch them to a soft diet of wet, mashed, or soaked food that is easier and less painful for them to eat.

Donkeys also need regular vaccinations against distemper, the flu, and tetanus. There may be other recommended vaccinations depending on the area you live in.

Like other equine and most outdoor animals, donkeys can suffer from intestinal parasites, particularly intestinal worms. Donkeys should have fecal checks about four times a year to look for parasites and treat them when found. Many medicines are not as effective as they used to be due to overuse and pest evolution, making it harder than it used to be to successfully treat many of these pests as they have developed resistance.

Because many pests have become resistant, you should have the animal checked after a course of treatment to ensure that it actually worked. Keeping your donkey's shelter and living space clean is the best way to avoid worms and other parasites, to begin with. Worms, like all parasites, have a unique life cycle that requires time for them to develop from one stage to the next. Regularly removing waste (largely donkey feces) a few times a week is a great way to reduce the animal's exposure to worm larva.

In the summer, you will want to groom the donkeys pretty much every day. In winter, you can scale it back to every other day. Air pockets naturally form in their coats, providing a degree of insulation from the cold, and brushing will break those air pockets.

Since donkeys have long, thick, coarse hair, it is much more prone to gathering dirt and debris than a horse, which is why they require more regular grooming. During the spring months (when the animals are molting their winter coats), you will need to groom them more often than usual to help get rid of the excess hair they are shedding.

Basic Tools

You don't need a ton of expensive specialty tools to keep your donkey looking and feeling good. Using a damp cloth, carefully clean any dirt or debris out of the animal's eyes, ear, nose, and mouth. This helps prevent infection and other issues that can result from dirt or debris build-up in these orifices.

A stiff round-headed brush made from metal, rubber, or plastic will be the most important tool to use for grooming your donkeys. Brush the animal with a body brush from head to tail, applying even pressure as you do so.

To keep the hooves clean and free from debris, you will need a hoof pick, which is an important grooming tool that allows you to remove safely and easily caked in gunk or debris. When cleaning the hooves, work from heel to toe, making sure you get all the crevices clean. You will want to keep an eye out for the back of the hoof (called the frog), turning black or even oozing. This indicates a bacterial infection called *thrush*, and it will need to be addressed immediately.

Keep your grooming tools clean, as this will help prevent the spread of germs. After each use, sanitize the grooming equipment using a mild detergent and warm water. You can let them air dry until their next use.

A basic grooming kit for donkeys will include a coarse curry comb brush, which is good for breaking up clumps of mud or debris. A short-bristled curry comb is an excellent all-purpose comb that can be used in most areas of the body for general brushing. Groomers gloves may be worn, but most animals prefer being groomed bare-handed, so this isn't required and is more of preference. A hoof hook will be needed for cleaning the coat.

A lot of donkey owners will use a rain rot prevention spray, insect repellent (especially for flies), and a coat conditioner of some sort to help keep their coats in good repair. All of these products can be bought from most outdoor farm stores, or you can even make your own. Skin conditioners are the most common product people make at home because it only requires basic ingredients. You can also make your own rain rot prevention and insect repellent, and recipes for these can easily be found online. Since skin conditioner is so easy to make, let's consider a recipe kindly provided by the Donkey Listener.

The Donkey Listener's Skin Conditioner

½ cup apple cider vinegar

½ cup water

3 drops of peppermint essential oil

3 drops of essential oil of your choice of scent

1 tbsp vitamin E oil

Mix all these ingredients and shake well before each use.

Clipping Donkeys

Occasionally, like most animals, a donkey may need a bit of a coat trim. Their coats are incredibly important to their bodily comfort and should never be fully trimmed. Their coats allow them to regulate their temperature properly and helps to protect against insect pests, especially flies, which pester pretty much all farm animals.

Sometimes, elderly or ill donkeys will experience a condition that causes an excessive overgrowth of their coat, leaving them matted and tangled, which can be painful and make the animal more prone to skin conditions. A donkey is most likely to need a coat clipping in late spring and early summer. This differs greatly from horses, which tend to be clipped in the winter.

Most donkeys need not be clipped often, but there are certain conditions and issues that can make this a necessity more often than is typical. Sometimes, donkeys will experience a greater than usual amount of hair growth during a winter, and they may be slow to molt the excess hair in the spring. When this happens, targeted light trimming is a great way to help the donkey's natural process along.

Certain skin conditions or a wound may also necessitate clipping a donkey to keep the area free of hair and debris. Many donkeys will experience lice infestations, which can often be addressed by bathing but may require some clipping in really severe cases. There are a variety of pest control products you can use that will make a lice infestation less likely to occur.

Hooves

The hooves of your donkeys are vital and keeping them healthy and in good shape is part and parcel to keeping your animals in top shape. Any time you groom your donkeys, you will want to clean out their hooves and check for any signs of injury or possible infection.

As we have noted a couple of times, it will be necessary to trim your donkey's hooves about every 4-8 weeks to keep them from becoming overgrown. You should only do this yourself if you have the proper tools and know-how.

Show Donkeys

Though not something commonly is known, some people keep donkeys as show animals, and these will require a much higher level of grooming than animals kept for work or milk. For show donkeys, you will want to bathe them regularly, and grooming will be more complex than it is with regular donkeys. You will need to clip the coat more often than a work donkey to keep it in good shape, and as a result, they will need to wear a rug in winter and perhaps even on cooler summer days.

Before a showing, it is advised to clip the donkey about once a week to allow unevenly shorn hair to grow back and look less shaggy. Using scissors with long blades and round ends is a good way to reduce uneven trimming and unsightly shag. The longer the blades of the scissors, the more even and smooth the resulting cut will look.

People who show their donkeys will also use hoof polish to make the hooves shine.

Chapter 8: Donkey Breeding

Though not as common as they once were, there are still places today where donkeys are used for transport, hauling cargo, and as the primary beast of burden for agriculture or small-scale industry. They are becoming more attractive today due to their hardiness and the low level of inputs required when compared to other equine species. They are more resilient for traction than oxen power, which can make them a more attractive animal for agricultural work than oxen.

Jennies and horse mares are similar with reproduction, but there are some key differences. The same is true for jacks and stallions - overall, the process is roughly similar, but there are some important differences that will affect breeding.

Basic Reproduction

A donkey reaches "puberty" at around two-years old, and jennies are in estrus (heat) for shorter periods of time than most horses. The estrus cycle in jennies tends to last between 23-30 days. Estrus itself, at its peak, lasts between 6-9 days, and jenny will be ovulating for about 5-6 days after the onset of estrus.

Jennies can be in heat more often than horses, which is beneficial for breeding since jacks can be finicky about mating. This means that the jenny has more opportunities to conceive than her horse counterpart.

Common symptoms of jennies in estrus include:

- Standing with legs apart in what is often called the breeding position.
- Excessive urination
- Tail raising
- Winking
- Drooling

The gestation cycle for a pregnant jenny is typically about 372-374 days, so a little over a year. Foal heat, or heat after the birth of a foal, sets in within 3-13 days after the jenny has given birth.

Jennies are extremely protective of their young and typically have a strong maternal instinct than mares do. You should keep this in mind when considering how you will go about socializing and handling foals. Jennies need to be comfortable with you in order to let you near their offspring, so you may have to socialize her and get her comfortable with you before you can safely touch the foal if this process of socialization wasn't already performed.

Jennies have a higher rate of fertility than horse mares, which makes them more likely to conceive. The conception rate for jennies is about 78%, compared with about 65% for mares.

A jenny is more likely to have multiple ovulatory periods than a mare, which makes the phenomena of twinning more common in them. This will need to be addressed by a vet, as twinnings present greatly increased risk of complications for the jenny. One embryo is typically destroyed for the safety of the jenny and to increase the likelihood that she will carry her pregnancy to term and birth a healthy foal.

Since jennies have narrower and longer, often protruding vaginas than mares, it can be more difficult to artificially inseminate a jenny than it is a mare. This can also put them at more risk for issues like cervical lesions and may have a harder time giving birth than a mare, which is why someone should be present when a jenny goes into labor.

We noted the signs above of a jenny in heat, and they are obvious, so it will be somewhat easy to know when she is ready to breed. The sound of braying jacks is said to cause them to go into heat faster. Jennies also become more vocal while in estrus than at any other time. If your jenny is more talkative than usual, this may be a sign that she is ready to breed.

As we noted above, jacks have a similar reproductive system to stallions, but there are some key differences. For one, the penis on a jack is larger than that of a similarly-sized horse. This means that if you geld any of your jacks, be aware that they will bleed more than horses tend to.

Accessory sex glands are also larger in jacks than in stallions. Unlike horses, it takes donkeys longer to achieve an erection and climax, about 15-30 minutes, compared to about 10 minutes for stallions. Jacks use something akin to foreplay, called teasing, with the jenny to "get in the mood." Breeding attempts, due to the time it can take for the jack to get ready and do its thing, maybe unsuccessful and take multiple tries. It should also be noted that the entire process can last as long as a couple of hours.

Young jacks will have a libido lower than their horse counterparts and won't reach sexual maturity for a few years after puberty.

Jacks can use artificial donkey vaginas, and this is a way to obtain sperm for artificial insemination, which is often the preferred method of breeders. It can be safer for the jenny, with a longer and narrower cervix than a horse mare.

Donkeys can be bred naturally, bred on a schedule, or bred via artificial insemination. Jacks and jennies can be kept together and allowed to "do what nature requires," or you can put the animals together at a specific time when the jenny is in the optimal state to conceive.

In natural systems, the jenny is most likely to conceive during what is called standing heat, referring to a 48-hour period after the onset of estrus.

Mule Breeding

A mule is a cross between a jack with a female mare (we will devote a short chapter to the mule below), and the pairing is not a natural one, but rather one that must be contrived or coaxed. If you want to breed jacks and horse mares, it is best to raise the jack in the company of horse mares and not jennies, as they will prefer their natural mate over horse mares. Raising the jack with horse mares will not only get him used to being in their presence; they will be his only source of "relief" for an exciting jack.

Jacks that are brought up in horse-like environments are far more likely to be receptive to breeding horse mares, but it will still have to be encouraged. Some have noted that farms with multiple jacks used for breeding with horse mares may encourage new jacks to mate with mares more readily. But, as we stated, you will have to cultivate a jack to breed with horse mares, and it isn't usually possible to have a jack that will mate with both horse mares and jennies. You will need to use separate animals for these purposes. To breed a specific jack with both horse mares and jennies, artificial insemination is the best route.

Mares are also not naturally drawn to jacks, and this can lead to distress at the presence of a braying jack. This further illustrates the importance of early socialization between the jack and mare. This will be less likely to happen between a pair that was raised together. A mare won't always stand to be mounted by a jack, and sometimes, she might even kick the jack, potentially injuring him as he tries to mount.

Restraints called breeding chutes or hobbles are often used to help ensure the safety of both animals in the process.

Breeding Miniature Donkeys

Miniature donkeys are affectionate and cute animals that have become increasingly popular as pets. These are much smaller than a standard donkey, standing no more than 36 inches tall. Besides being cute and having great temperaments, miniature donkeys also don't require as much space or input due to their smaller size.

Their size does present a limitation in the amount of work they can do, the amount of weight they can hold, and the size of rider appropriate for their stature. You will want to remember this when considering breeding miniatures as if you are breeding for work animals; the miniature is not likely the best choice.

The first thing you will need to do is find a jack and jenny that are good representations of the miniature breed in terms of size, coat, having long, straight legs, and so on. A jenny with wider hips and ribcage will have an easier time giving birth than one with more narrow hips and ribs.

You will want to have a potential breeding pair checked out by a vet to ensure they are healthy and have no diseases they could transmit in the process of breeding. Both Jenny and Jack should be at least three years old before any attempts of breeding begin. This is to make sure that both animals are fully sexually developed.

Wash both animals before bringing them together, and many people will pin up the jennies' tail to make it easier for the jack to mount her. It is recommended to wash their genitals with iodine soap to ensure that both are free of any bacteria or potentially harmful pathogens.

You may need to hold or restrain the jenny while the jack sniffs and inspects her. It is an important part of the mating process for jacks, but it has a tendency to make the jenny a bit nervous. If her tail isn't already tied back, a receptive jenny will raise it up to indicate her interest.

Once the breeding process is complete, you will want to separate the pair and release the jenny's tail if it was tied up. The jenny should be taken to a quiet, calm place for the year (roughly) it takes her to gestate a foal. Keeping the jenny calm and stress-free will help ensure she has a healthy pregnancy.

A pregnant jenny shouldn't be exercised vigorously, but she should be encouraged to move around each day when she feels the desire.

During the last three months of pregnancy, you will want to increase the amount you feed the pregnant jenny by about 50% to account for the needs of her growing foal. In the last month of her pregnancy, place the jenny in a foaling stall, which is specially designed to be away from other animals and provide her a safe and private space to give birth.

The foaling stall should be covered with clean thick bedding made from straw or wood shavings (straw is preferable). It is important that the jenny be away from other animals and as far away from loud noise as possible; she should be kept in as little stress as possible during labor. While known for being affectionate, jennies about to give birth are less friendly shortly before entering labor, so if your usually-loving jenny cops a bit of an attitude, it is a good sign that she is going to give birth soon.

About 48-hours before giving birth, you will notice the jenny's udders begin to swell, and there may even be a slightly waxy secretion coming out of her teats. This is perfectly normal.

You will want to be nearby when the jenny goes into labor in case you need to provide assistance but try to give her as much space as possible, so she doesn't feel crowded or confined. You don't want to cause her any unnecessary stress. This can prolong the time it takes for her to give birth and increase the chances of complications. She will begin to roll around and pace the stall right before she gives birth.

Once the jenny's water breaks, the foal will begin its appearance; further contractions will allow her to push the baby the rest of the way out. This can take a little while, but if about 20 minutes pass by with no progress or contractions, it is best to call in a vet to see if there are issues with her pregnancy that you aren't suited to handle.

After the foal is born, the jenny will sever the umbilical cord herself and clean the foal. The foal, if healthy, should stand shortly thereafter and begin to nurse. Though not all that common, sometimes jennies fear their foal at first. If this happens and she won't let the foal nurse, hold and comfort the jenny until the foal can approach the jenny and nurse.

If possible, have both the jenny and the foal examined by a vet a few days after the birth. This will allow the vet to determine that both mom and baby are in good condition. The vet will look for any remaining placenta that may need to be removed, as well as signs of mastitis. This is an inflammation of the teats that can lead to discomfort and even the avoidance of nursing and should be quickly addressed. There are a lot of different treatments that are effective for mastitis.

The vet will also check to make sure the foal is getting an adequate supply of milk. If the foal cannot get enough milk from the jenny, it may be recommended that you give the foal supplemental food to make up for calories and needed nutrients it isn't receiving from its mother.

Chapter 9: Donkey Milking (and Why You Should Consider It)

Milk probably isn't the first thing you associate with donkeys. Yet, donkey milk is becoming a lucrative field; it may be, perhaps, something you consider becoming involved with if you are going to raise donkeys. Donkey milk has been used since ancient times for a wide range of uses and is becoming popular again today.

In fact, donkey milk is becoming a highly sought ingredient for a number of different health and beauty products. This has led to a dramatic rise in the price the milk fetches on the open market. Prices can be as high as about $50 a liter, which is, indeed, an extremely high price for milk!

Benefits of Donkey Milk

In ancient times, donkey milk was used medicinally to treat many different ailments and as a beauty enhancer. Legend states that Cleopatra, the famous Queen of Egypt, took baths in donkey milk to help maintain her youthful appearance and glowing skin. Modern science shows that there is a lot to this legend, even if it didn't happen as historical fact.

It was long used as a medicine for a range of ailments from an upset stomach to allergies.

We have numerous ancient accounts for the use of donkey milk beyond the Cleopatra legend. The father of medicine, Hippocrates, writes one of the oldest known accounts about the benefits of donkey milk. Also, ancient Roman records attest to its fairly widespread use. Napoleon's sister is known to have included it in her skin care regimen. Also, in France, donkey milk was used until the twentieth century to feed orphaned infants and as a cure for the sick and elderly.

Common Uses of Donkey Milk Today

Even today, some people still argue for the medicinal value of donkey milk, claiming it can help people with issues such as bronchitis or asthma. This should not replace modern medical treatment and medication, and a lot more study needs to be done to determine the true efficacy of donkey milk as a good treatment for these conditions.

People with severe allergies may benefit from the consumption of donkey milk. Many people claim that by simply drinking a little milk each day, they saw dramatic reductions in their allergy symptoms. Like with other health claims made about donkey milk, there needs to be more research to determine how well it actually works for these conditions and to understand what it is about this type of milk that makes it useful.

Serbia is one of the largest producing regions for donkey milk and what is considered to be the most expensive cheese in the world - made from donkey milk - is produced there at Zasavica Nature Reserve. The cheese sells for about $48 euros per 50 grams of cheese. Indeed, pricey, with a unique taste and texture that people swear cannot be rivaled by other types of specialty cheese. Other nations with decent-sized donkey milk production capabilities include South Korea, Belgium, and Switzerland.

Scientific studies have shown that, chemically, donkey milk is the closest to human breast milk and is lower in fat and much higher in Omega-3 fatty acids than cow's milk. There have been recent studies published in the professional journal, <u>Current Pharmaceutical Design</u>, that demonstrates_that_donkey milk has the ability to dilate blood vessels and can reduce the hardening of arteries. Another recent piece in the <u>Journal of Food Science</u> has described donkey milk as a "pharmafood" for its myriad of benefits in terms of both health and nutrition.

More and more, donkey milk is used in skin products helpful in treating a variety of skin conditions like psoriasis and eczema. It is also safe for use on overly sensitive skin and can be made into a gentle soap. Some say that donkey milk contains anti-aging properties, and its fat content makes it great at skin hydration, helping improve the look and elasticity of the skin. It is also known as a great skin cleanser.

This milk can also be beneficial for infants that suffer from gastric issues since, at a chemical structural level, it is so close to human breast milk. It is also high in much-needed vitamins and minerals, and it may be a better alternative than formula or cow's milk. Donkey milk has a comparable level of protein to cow's milk but is much higher in vitamin C.

As more research continues to identify the widely varied benefits of donkey milk, many expect to continue to see it rise in popularity and demand.

Considerations

In terms of animals that can be milked, the donkey isn't high on the list of good sources since they produce so little milk. While donkey milk, when compared to that of cow's milk, is far more scarce, it is used for far more specialized purposes than cow milk, so the scarcity isn't as much of an issue as it might immediately seem.

Because they produce so little milk, specialty products are the most common that use this unique and rare substance. Jennies can only be milked for about 2-3 months after giving birth. They rarely produce more than about 400 mL of milk a day, a very tiny amount when compared to cows.

Chapter 10: Identifying and Preventing Donkey Diseases

The donkey is known and prized for being a hardy and durable creature, but this does not mean they never suffer from health issues. Their hardiness is, of course, one reason they were so popular historically and one of the main reasons they are growing in popularity today. However, even though they are hardy and can live in challenging environments, they remain faced with the risk of several different health problems.

As we noted earlier, donkeys tend to hide their emotions, and this is also true when they are ill. There is a good chance your donkey won't display obvious symptoms of illness until the illness has progressed to a point where it is impossible for the animal to hide any longer. This can often result in letting something small and simple fester to where it becomes a larger issue.

Basic Health Considerations

The more time you spend with your donkeys, the better your relationship and understanding of them will be. It will also help you to learn the personality, temperament, and particular behaviors of each animal, which can make it a lot easier to tell when something isn't quite right with them. It is highly recommended that you do regular body checks to look for any potential issues and address them as soon as you notice anything. These checks are great to do in tandem with daily grooming.

Common Donkey Ailments and Their Symptoms

Like any animal, donkeys can get a wide range of diseases that can be mild to even life-threatening. What follows are some of the most common ailments that donkeys suffer from, and symptoms associated with these conditions.

Abscesses

An abscess is caused when an outside source – often a pathogen or an injury – spurs the overproduction of white blood cells, which can lead to painful sores, which then rupture and exude pus. An abscess can show up in any number of places on the donkey from inside the body, in the mouth, or even on the hooves. They can rupture, causing the expulsion of a large amount of unpleasant smelling pus.

If left untreated, especially on the hooves, it can lead to chronic sores and an infection that can spread up into surrounding tissues, causing a lot of discomfort and even risking permanent damage. You will need to consult a vet to diagnose and properly treat abscesses.

The abscess may be lanced, and a sample checked for bacteria that could necessitate the need for a course of antibiotics. The wound may also be irrigated or deeply cleaned to help avoid future infection and to aid in the healing of the wound.

Anthrax

Anthrax spores are commonly found in soils in most areas of the world. Known as Bacillus anthracis, this toxin can lay dormant in the soil for many years, becoming "activated" during certain climatic conditions such as cool and wet weather that is immediately followed by very hot and dry weather. The spores can live in the soil for as long as 48 years!

Animals can then eat grass that has been contaminated with anthrax spores and become ill. Common symptoms of anthrax include mood changes like depression, lack of physical coordination, uncontrollable tremors, and even random bleeding. You will want to contact the vet immediately if they display any of these systems and may have been exposed to contaminated soil as it can be fatal.

Anthrax is highly spreadable and can easily be spread from an infected donkey to other animals and even humans. This is why any confirmed cases of anthrax must be reported to appreciate local government officials.

There is a vaccine available to inoculate against anthrax, and it is highly recommended, particularly if you live in an area where anthrax has been known to be found. If caught early, anthrax poisoning can be treated with antibiotics, but since the toxin can often prove fatal, it is better to rely on the vaccination.

Arthritis

Like humans, donkeys can suffer from arthritis as they get older. Arthritis is also caused by certain genetic predispositions and can also be caused by poor nutrition and inadequate space. The symptoms of arthritis in donkeys can vary but most commonly include changes in the animal's gait, swollen joints, weight loss, and changes in the condition of their coat.

There are a variety of ways to treat arthritis in donkeys, but the proper course of treatment will depend on the underlying cause of the arthritis. You will want to contact a vet on the appropriate treatment plan for your animal.

Especially for older animals, you may have to modify their environment to make it safer and easier for an arthritic animal to get around. This can include reducing the grade of the terrain if it is steep, moving food and water closer to where the donkey spends its time, and more. A donkey with arthritis can still live a long and happy life; it just takes a bit of ingenuity to figure out ways to make life easier on the animal.

Brucellosis

This condition typically presents in *poll evil* (a painful condition) and *fistulous withers* (another inflammatory condition). The poll of the donkey refers to the space between the ears down to the back of its neck. Poll evil occurs when this area is injured and swells, becoming inflamed and infected. This can lead to the waning and even the necrosis (death) of the affected tissue.

Fistulous withers refers to a similar condition in which the supraspinous bursa (which is located near the withers of the animal) becomes infected. This can occur because of an injury or an infection, most commonly Brucella abortus, hence the name of the condition.

Symptoms of these conditions include swelling, noticeable tenderness, heat emitting from the area, new sensitivities in the animal, as well as fever and listlessness. The bursa, if left untreated, can rupture and leak infectious fluid.

Both poll evil and fistulous withers can be treated, but if left untreated, they can easily turn into chronic conditions that can lead to even further inflammation and permanent scar tissues.

Bursas that haven't ruptured are often treated with antibiotics. A ruptured bursa is treated by removing tissue in the affected area and cleaning the area with a betadine solution. A course of antibiotics will also often be given to help ensure that all infection has been killed off.

Donkeys do not spread this condition to other animals nor to humans, so no separation or extra caution will need to be taken. It should be noted that cows suffering from these conditions can spread it to other animals, though.

Cataracts

This is another common issue that plagues both aging humans and donkeys alike. It is marked by the increasing opacity of the lens of the eyeball, which reduces sight. This is often a congenital issue that develops in the animal as it ages. However, it can also be caused because of trauma, radiation, toxins, or other eye conditions.

The issue is most noticeable by the steady increase in the cloudiness and grayness of the lens of the eye. You will want to contact your vet to determine the source and treatment for cataracts. Surgery is the only known cure for cataracts, but this can also lead to permanent vision loss – but either way, cataracts may cause blindness in the end.

If surgery isn't recommended or doesn't seem like a good option, you may need to modify their surroundings to make it easier for a poorly-sighted animal to get around, eat, and drink with relative ease.

Conjunctivitis

This is a common condition in donkeys that is often a result of an injury to the eye. Virus and fungal infections are another cause of this condition. Eye irritants like dust and dirt can also lead to minor cases. This occurs because of the inner eyelid and surrounding soft tissue becoming inflamed.

Symptoms include redness and swelling around the eyes, often with a mucus-like discharge coming from the eye.

Treatments for this condition will depend on the source of the irritation. If the issue results from an eye irritant or foreign body, you will want to flush the eye with water thoroughly. In the event of this being caused by fungal infections, viruses, or injury, you will want to contact the vet to determine the proper course of action.

Cystitis and Pyelonephritis

Cystitis is a common type of equine urinary tract infection. Infections like this are most often a result of some condition that is restricting the flow of urine and may result from bacteria such as E. coli Enterococcus app, or Streptococcus app.

Pyelonephritis is a urinary tract infection that has spread to the kidneys and gotten more severe.

The symptoms most commonly associated with these conditions are similar to human experiences, including frequent urination and blood in the urine. If the infection has spread to the kidneys, they may begin losing weight and exhibiting certain behavior changes, like depression.

You will need to contact your vet for proper diagnosis and treatment of either of these issues. While you are waiting to take the animal in, make sure they stay well hydrated, as this can help reduce the severity of some of the symptoms.

Colic

This is actually a more general term than the name of a specific condition. The word simply refers to abdominal or stomach pain and discomfort and can be a result of a variety of different issues. Colic can often be detected by sounds from the gut, an increased heart rate, and even increased respiration.

Impaction is a type of colic that results from something in the gut, most often undigested food. Cramps are called spasmodic colic and often cause general discomfort. Flatulent colic is a fancy name for stomach or gastrointestinal discomfort that results from excess gas. Tumors, which are most often seen in older animals, may also be a cause of colic. Torsion is a very painful condition in which the donkey has a twisted gut, which will naturally cause a lot of pain. Ulcers may also be a source. Worms, such as tapeworms or roundworms, will also commonly cause colic. Pancreatitis, which is caused by the swelling and inflammation of the pancreas, can also result in colic and can be a serious issue.

Most often, the donkey will display symptoms such as a refusal to eat. There are a variety of ways that this condition can be treated, from treating the underlying cause or even providing the animal with additional fluids through a tube in the nose. An intravenous drip may also supply the animal with extra fluids. In rare cases, colic can necessitate surgery and may even be fatal.

Dirty or inadequate water can be a cause of colic and issues with the feed. This is especially true if you change the animal's diet suddenly, without allowing them to become acclimatized to the new food gradually. Grazing on sandy soils may cause colic and eating non-food materials like rope, wood, plastic, or other materials.

The diseases and ailments we have listed here are, of course, not an exhaustive list of conditions that can affect donkeys, but they do cover the range of the most common issues that they are likely to experience. The longer you raise and care for these animals, the more familiar you will get with some of the main issues that may be a problem with these animals, what to do, and when to call in a vet or other professional.

Chapter 11: A Word On Mules

Mules are, for all intents and purposes, a hybrid creature. Many confuse donkeys with mules, but they are different. Donkeys descended from wild asses in Africa and Asia, whereas a mule is a cross between a female horse and a jack.

There are also crosses between male horses and jennies, but these are called hinnies. They are very similar to mules but are a bit smaller and shouldn't be confused for the same animal.

A mule is a unique animal genetically, being a cross between a horse with 64 chromosomes and a donkey that has 62. Both mules and hinnies have 63 chromosomes, making them incredibly unique.

Basically, this means that mules and hinnies are sterile and unable to reproduce sexually. The female mule, called a molly or a molly mule, has an estrus cycle, which would make it theoretically possible for her to conceive. Still, since males are usually 99.9% sterile, there are few records of any actual pregnancies or births among mollies - most often, the rare birth of a foal results from an embryo transfer. The mule is desirable because they tend to be healthier and much hardier than comparably-sized horses and require less food and care.

Similarities and Differences Between Mules and Standard Donkeys

Though they are easily confused for donkeys, a mule actually has more physically in common with a horse than a donkey. When it comes to body size, shape, teeth, and more, they are morphologically more similar to the mare than the jack. There are different types of mules, including miniatures. A typical mule, because of the horse side of their genetics, is a bit larger than a standard donkey.

Donkeys have very long ears, which is one of the most clearly identifiable features of the animal. However, a mule will have ears that are smaller and more like a horse than a donkey.

Vocalizations are another significant way to distinguish between a donkey and a mule. A donkey is well known for its hee-haw call, whereas a mule has something that is more between a whinny and the hee-haw. It is a distinctive sound that isn't likely to be confused with a donkey – once you are used to it.

Mules, like donkeys and horses, are long-lived animals and typically live between 30-40 years, though working or breeding animals may have shorter lifespans.

One of the things that make mules more attractive to some than donkeys is that they are more intelligent - which says a lot, seeing as how donkeys have amazing intelligence, as well. Mules also seem a bit less stubborn than donkeys; mules, quickly pick up skills, more like horse, than do the thoughtful and cautious donkeys.

A mule will typically weigh between 800-1000 pounds, but miniatures can be so small as to weigh less than 50 pounds. Miniature mules are super cute and sweet creatures that make great pets or companion animals.

Though half-descended from a mare, the skin of a mule isn't nearly as sensitive as horse skin; it is more like donkey skin, resistant to both sun and rain, making them a hardier animal than their horse counterparts. This doesn't, of course, mean they require no shelter from the elements, but rather that they are less sensitive and more adaptable to their environment than a horse is.

Like a donkey, a mule is better for navigating complex and uneven terrain. They have hooves much harder than horses, and thus they are much less likely to crack and can handle rocky or uneven terrain. Since they don't typically have shoes, they are easier and less expensive to care for than horses.

Just as with donkeys and horses, the mule is a great animal for carrying small loads. They can carry about 20% of their body weight on their backs and much more when pulling a cart over the ground.

Just like a donkey, a mule is not a horse, even if half of its genetics come from them. They have very different nutritional needs and requirements and shouldn't be treated as a small horse, but rather a unique creature in their own right.

As with donkeys, mules' digestive system is far better suited to pasture that is of low nutritional value. It takes them longer to digest their food, which allows them to get as many nutrients as possible from feeding. Food that is too rich or high in nutrients can cause a range of gastrointestinal issues, just like it will with donkeys.

You will need to remember that they do not share the same requirements as horses and, in terms of maintenance and care, and are more akin to the donkey side of their ancestry – and should be dealt with as such.

Feeding a mule should be approached in the same way you would approach feeding a donkey. Their food needs to be appropriate for their nutritional and digestive needs, and the amount that they eat needs to be controlled. Like donkeys, mules are known to overeat when given an overabundance of food, and this can cause problems like obesity (or even diabetes), which mules are more susceptible to than horses.

Never use equipment meant for horses with mules. While they have a similar body type, they aren't the same, and using inappropriate gear can harm and injure the animal. If at all possible, get halters and other equipment especially suited for mules. There are many places where you can have a custom halter, or other equipment made that is exactly to size for your animal. Though this is more expensive than buying a halter from a farm store, it will fit better and likely lead to better results with the animal.

Mules, like both donkeys and horses, come in a wide range of sizes and colors, and what will work best for you will depend on the intended use of the animal and your personal preferences. A mule comes with a heftier price tag than a donkey since it is a crossbreed, and it takes more skill to breed and raise them. You can expect to pay somewhere between $1,200-5,000 for a mule, perhaps more if you are looking at getting a miniature.

Interesting Facts About Mules

Militaries around the world have long relied on mules as they are hardier, require fewer inputs, and can handle a more diverse range of terrains and environments than horses can. They are cheaper and easier to care for and maintain, making them superior to the horse for many applications.

The mule has even been used in more modern warfare. In the 80s, when the US army was working in Afghanistan, mules were used to carry weapons and supplies over the harsh terrain. Estimates are that as many as 10,000 mules were used in these operations.

There is a long historical tradition of both mules and donkeys being used in wars, from ancient warfare to major world wars. They made better assistants than horses because they require less food and other inputs, are tougher, and can navigate a diverse range of terrain types, whereas horses need to have smooth, flat ground, which can't always be found in a warzone.

Mules are predominately bred in China and Mexico, though there are known breeders on almost every continent and in every country.

Like the donkey, a mule will resort to kicking when threatened. They can kick both front and backward, but it's unusual that they can also kick sideways – certainly something that many people don't expect to see when dealing with these animals. Their hind legs are amazingly strong, and a good kick can both hurt and do serious damage. Keep this in mind when dealing with mules and try to steer clear of those powerful back legs!

Breeding and Raising Mules

We touched on some of the basics for breeding mules in the chapter on reproduction. The cross between a horse mare and a jack is not the easiest to produce since donkeys and horses, being different species, don't mate naturally. The exception is apparently with jacks that are raised *exclusively* with horses. It is far easier to get a jack – raised with horses only, rather than with other donkeys or a mix of both - to breed with mares, as it seems more natural to them.

Donkeys and horses have similar but different sexual reproduction systems and different ways of approaching breeding, which makes it more difficult to have successful intercourse, but it is not impossible. Many people choose to use artificial insemination as the key means for reproduction as it is easier to accomplish and requires a lot less effort on everyone's part. However, as we noted in the chapter about breeding, it is not impossible, and with some know-how and skill, you can get mares and jacks to breed naturally.

As we also noted, most male mules are sterile, though females are still known to go into heat and, on rare occasions, give birth to a foal. Most often, though, they cannot reproduce, and thus the only way to get a mule is through the direct breeding of horse mares and jacks.

Though they have the morphology more akin to a horse, their care is more akin to the donkey portion of their genetics. They can live in a far more diverse range of environments than horses can, and their hooves are much more like a donkey than a horse, making them easier to care for and less demanding - shoes are not usually necessary for mules. Their dietary needs are very similar to their donkey counterparts.

They need to be fed on high fiber vegetation or supplemental hay or straw that is low in sugar. Rich forage or nutrient-dense vegetation is not ideal for those animals. For the best results in terms of proper nutrition, please consult the chapter on feeding donkeys for more information.

For best results when training your mule, get involved with them as soon as possible after they are born. The earlier you can start to socialize them, the better your relationship with them will be, and the easier they will be to train. Since they are a little less thoughtful and contemplative than donkeys, they tend to pick up on skills and training a little faster, but like the donkey, they don't need as much repetition to learn the task as a horse would.

You can develop something closely akin to a friendship with a mule, just as you can with a donkey, and this is not only regarding, but makes it easier to give them the care they need. Since they, like donkeys, aren't as expressive as horses, knowing them well makes it easier to read their emotions and body language. This is especially important if the animal is sick or injured. They enjoy social interaction with people and other animals, and as a result, they may make a better companion animal than a donkey.

Your mule's body language should not be read exactly as a horse's body language; mules are likely to display different emotions or desires. They may approach humans with their ears turned back, which, like a horse, is an indication of aggravation or aggression. But in a mule, it could mean they are asking for a treat. It takes time to get to know what the different body cues mean, and it helps to consider what the rest of the body is doing and the context the action is taking place in. That will help you better determine what their desires or intentions are.

Mules are territorial in much the same way as donkeys are, and this can be both a good and a bad thing. Like the donkey, a mule can be trained to watch over the livestock and chase predators. However, also like the donkey, they are not fans of any canine species, so their interaction with a family dog may be less than ideal. Whether you are raising and keeping donkeys or mules, use caution when letting a dog near them.

Mules have a different smell than either a donkey or a horse, and this can lead to some confusion if mules are kept with other types of equine. It seems the other animals have a harder time figuring out what exactly the mule is. Mules can be kept with other mules, horses, donkeys, or livestock. They are versatile animals that can take on a range of jobs on a farm and simply keep a person company.

A mule, like a donkey, will require regular grooming to keep them in good shape. Their coat is smoother than a donkey but caring for it is very similar. They need regular brushing to get rid of mud and other debris that collects in their fur. They will also need to have their eyes, ears, mouth, and hooves cleaned out regularly in the same manner as a donkey. Like a donkey, their hooves continue to grow throughout their lives and will need to be trimmed regularly, but they do not need shoes or the same level environment a horse requires.

Conclusion

Donkeys are unique and hardy creatures that evolved to live in harsh and unforgiving environments. As a result, they are prized for their relatively low-maintenance care, good demeanor, and hard work ethic. These animals, when cared for and trained properly, can perform several functions from being ridden to protecting livestock.

Raising donkeys can also be a lucrative business idea as the donkey is ideal for certain activities and environments. As we close this brief guide to owning and raising donkeys, let's look at a couple of ways you can turn to raise donkeys into a lucrative money-making venture that provides a valuable service and is rewarding for both you and the donkey.

Since donkeys are such emotional and social creatures, some raise donkeys, particularly miniatures, to be petted. Since they are small and very friendly, miniature donkeys are great family animals for people with a small amount of land and a desire for a companion animal less common than the humble dog. If you are raising donkeys and selling them to be pets, you will want to do your homework when determining who to sell animals to.

As we noted numerous times in this guide, donkeys are long-lived animals, and anyone who is interested in adopting one needs to understand this, and the fact that they require some specialized care; they are not cared for exactly like horses. You might do background checks or even checking out the property of potential owners to ensure that they are a good fit for owning a donkey (or donkeys) as pets.

Since these animals are so social, anyone interested in buying one as a pet needs to know just how much time and socialization is necessary for their animal to be happy and fulfilled. Many get a pair of donkeys so they can keep each other company and maybe a suggestion to give a potential adopter of donkeys.

You will need to check with your local government offices to learn of the rules and regulations required for selling donkeys as pets and ensure that you follow the proper channels of providing equine passports for any donkey you sell.

Some people will raise and sell donkeys as light work animals. Though this isn't as common as it once was, donkeys are a great investment for a variety of different work activities, from agricultural work to hauling goods or people. Many tourist locations use donkeys to carry the packs of hikers or even for tourists to ride to a particular destination (recall the Grand Canyon, which relies on donkeys – especially mules). You may also want to check out your local laws to ensure that you are following all the rules and regulations that required for selling donkeys in your area.

Finally, this is perhaps the most lucrative way of using donkeys, and that is selling their milk. As we touched on in the chapter about donkey milk, it has been proven to be highly useful for a variety of conditions. People still use it to treat a variety of health ailments from eczema to allergies. More commonly, though, donkey milk is used in high-end beauty products.

Known and lauded for its myriad of benefits to the skin, such as anti-aging properties, advanced hydration, and the ability of people even with sensitive skin to use products made from donkey milk, beauty products made with it are becoming increasingly popular. Due to the high demand and the relative scarcity of donkey milk, the milk sells for a premium; cheese made from this milk can go for as high as $1,000 per pound, making it one of the most expensive milk products in the world.

Donkey milk is also used for a variety of other purposes, including giving it to sick or fussy children and even making cheese from it. The world's most expensive cheese is made from donkey milk.

Since donkeys don't produce large quantities of milk, you will need a decent number of animals to get enough milk to make it worth your while. Still, there is such high demand, and this might be the best business opportunity related to raising donkeys. Many farmers who raise donkeys for their milk work directly with a particular business or beauty company and sell their milk exclusively to said company. If you have enough animals, you may be able to produce enough milk to supply more than one small company. This isn't something that can be done on an industrial scale, and chances are, you will be servicing just one or two small companies.

Regardless of what you choose to use the donkeys for, they are great animals that provide a ton of work power and can even guard livestock. They are highly intelligent creatures who can adapt to a wide range of environments and can learn to perform a range of different skills, depending on your needs and expectations.

Understanding the emotional nature, temperament, and special needs of donkeys will make it easier to raise them healthily and happily. Keeping donkeys for any reason is a rewarding endeavor that allows you to develop a deep bond with an affectionate and loving creature that can also provide work power and more.

Raising healthy, happy, and well-trained donkeys will earn you a reputation far outside of your local area. People interested in buying donkeys will come from far and wide to obtain animals that have a solid pedigree and are from a trainer/owner who is well known for providing the animals with the best possible care, training, and socialization.

Donkeys may not be the most common animal anymore, but they have a long and storied history of living alongside humans. For some 6,000 years, donkey and man have lived and worked together in a variety of ways, working the narrow rows between vineyards or teaching a child how to ride.

They have evolved and been selectively bred to have several traits that make them more adaptable and useful to humans in a variety of climates and types of terrain. Donkeys are known for being affectionate and sweet to humans when they have been properly socialized. These are highly-intelligent creatures that need a decent amount of mental stimulation to keep them at their happiest and healthiest.

This guide has sought to provide those interested in raising donkeys, whether for commercial or personal reasons, the information they need to make an informed decision on the type of animal to get. It also covers the care they need, how to train them in basic skills, and an overview of different ailments common to the animals and how to spot or prevent these from occurring to begin with.

While this isn't a completely comprehensive guide, it should give you the knowledge you need to get started on your journey with the humble donkey. Given a bad reputation for being stubborn, this thoughtful animal just needs the right kind of training and can learn several skills and behaviors, providing you with companionship and animal power for many years to come.

Here's another book by Dion Rosser that you might like

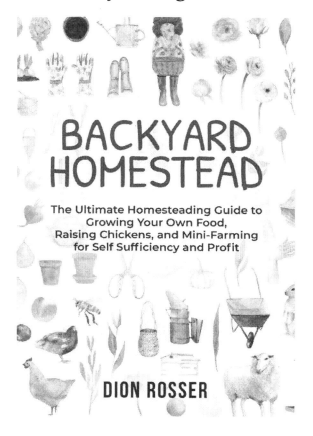

Made in the USA
Middletown, DE
07 June 2025

76669280R00060